Lasting

Poems on Aging

Edited by Meg Files

Pima Press

Tucson, Arizona

Published by Pima Press
Pima Community College
2202 West Anklam Road
Tucson, Arizona 85709-0170

 Supported by the Arizona Commission on the Arts with funding from the State of Arizona and the National Endowment for the Arts

[clmp] Member of the Council of Literary Magazines and Presses

Library of Congress Cataloging-in-Publication Data

Lasting : poems on aging / edited by Meg Files.— 1st ed.
    p. cm.
 ISBN-13: 978-1-931638-03-6 (pbk. : alk. paper)
 ISBN-10: 1-931638-03-9 (pbk. : alk. paper)
 1. Age groups—Poetry. 2. Old age—Poetry. 3. Aging—Poetry. 4. American poetry. I. Files, Meg, 1946-
 PS595.A33L37 2005
 811.008'0354—dc22
                         2005029497

Cover Art: "The Long Loneliness" by Frances O'Brien
Used by permission of the O'Brien estate
Production: Leila Joiner

Published in the United States of America
First edition: November 2005

ISBN 1-931638-03-9
ISBN 978-1-931638-03-6

Permission acknowledgments appear on pages 281-293 and constitute a continuation of the copyright page.

 PimaCommunityCollege

Contents

PART 2: BEING OLD, STILL PLAYING

PART 3: COMING TO THE SECRET NAMES OF STARS

ACKNOWLEDGMENTS

Introduction

RECENTLY I CAME upon a file folder I hadn't seen for thirty years. Labeled "Old Age," it was the repository of little notes to myself and quotes and clippings. This manila time capsule includes a letter from my mother reminding me—why? I wonder now—that "getting old sure beats the alternative." Neither of us knew then that she would die at 61. On blue paper I'd copied Dylan Thomas's lines: "Old age should burn and rave at close of day; / Rage, rage against the dying of the light." Here's a brittle article from a Sunday supplement on the health benefits of a positive attitude for "golden-agers." And a piece of advice to my future self: "If you have false teeth, wear them."

My file of mixed messages may mirror the general ambivalence. Hearing that I was editing a book of poems on the subject of aging, people had two distinct reactions: "Great! I need to read that" or "Who'd want to read such a downer of a book?"

Most people don't even know what words to use. In his poem "Assisted Living," Peter Meinke observes that "Language is queer: adult movies / mean fucking but adult centers / mean dying though both mean / without dignity in front of others."

In this book, poets have found the language to examine aging— and its non-alternative.

THE FIRST PART, "Looking at Aging Faces," offers views from outside. We learn, for instance, how approaching death can send us backward, perhaps to resist going forward. The father in Al Zolynas' poem "My Father, at the Age of Eighty-Three, Shows Up at the Family Reunion, Sporting an Amazing Beard" seems "no longer fit for this planet." "Nothing seems familiar," the son writes, "but the distant call, quiet and insistent, heard / like the murmur of wind in grass / or the ocean breaking on a shore."

Other poets also write about their aging parents. Sandra Gilbert notes her 97-year-old mother's insistence: "Listen, Sandra, / I'm still too young / to be shelved like this." How is it for our parents and for those left to interpret their aging, sometimes their dementia, their deaths? In Donald Finkel's "Leavings," a mother tries to escape her rest home: "*Some rest*, she wheezed, / and hailed a patrol car: *Take me to the Hilton, cabby.*" Groping for her purse she "felt her heart snap open, all but empty: / one lime LifeSaver, shrouded in lint, / two lichen-green pennies to rest on her eyes."

Some poems draw portraits of old people. (And they aren't all sweet or wise. In William Pitt Root's "Passing Go," an old woman gets out of paying bus fare by saying something, well, inappropriate.) Some portraits are dedications to other poets.

The last poems in this section look at what's to come. There are warnings about whom we don't want to become, like the "old man with huge ankles" in Jefferson Carter's poem "Foul Mouth" who snarls at his wife, "Help me, goddamit! I'm / the one who's dying." Tricia Cherin's "Role Models" presents a different, sadly optimistic approach, observing that "even last week's widows have newly washed hair / knowing already that fresh love / is their only hope." There's advice, such as Marge Piercy's in "The lived in look," about what to remember and what to let go: "This is the sweet imprint of your life / and loves upon the rumpled sheets / of your days. Relax. Breathe deeply. Mess will make us free."

The old woman in David St. John's "Grace Harbour" "believed those days she might live / Forever even though she knew better & why." All of us, knowing what's to come, might pray, as in Kim Addonizio's "Getting Older," that memory is enough "to last, if it has to, the rest of your life."

THE SECOND SECTION of the book, "Being Old, Still Playing," includes the most poems. Everyone, it seems, has plenty to say about the experiences of getting and being old.

The first poems examine what happens to the body. Ruth Stone captures the unnerving sense of change: "My true self has been stitched to another face." Bernardo Taiz almost proudly catalogs his changes: "Vascular system gridlocked, / vertebrae re-configured, / a foot of colon excised here, / a grand toe bonsai'd there." W.D. Snodgrass gets a pacemaker to "Keep this old lame dog synchronized, / Steady, sparked up, still in the race." Gary Soto says that these days "I have to help my body parts." Still, though—"Fellas, sour liver / And trusty kidney, I'm full of hope."

Poems about the body segue into explorations of what aging can do to the mind and memory, and then into poems about the effects of aging on long relationships, and then, quite naturally, into sex. Sam Hamill writes that an orchid blossoming is "Erotic because there's death / at the heart of birth." C.K. Williams notes the proximity: "Sex and death: how close / they can seem. / So constantly conscious now of death moving toward me, sometimes I / think I confound them." Tricia Cherin's poem "Last Fucks" observes that "somber abandon" is "such good practice / for the near oblivion."

This section ends with poems about enduring. In "Witness," Donald Hall reminds us that "Each September / day is the last day." Alicia Ostriker asks: "And when the clock says *Almost / Quitting time*, do you still answer *Never*?"

THE FINAL SECTION, "Coming to the Secret Names of Stars," is about final things: what will come, the finality of aging, death, and coming to terms with mortality. Peter Meinke's poem "The Death of Friends" faces—despite the stories we try to tell ourselves about how we go on after death—the absolute finality. Still, poets cannot help contemplating an afterlife, as in Maxine Kumin's "Summer Meditation": "If only death could be / like going to the movies. / You get up afterward / and go out / saying, how was it?"

TAKEN TOGETHER, the poems become a conversation, with questions and answers, with the exchange and play of fine talk—Peter Meinke's finality, people absolutely blipped out, and then Philip Levine's *Yes, but*: at the end "taking nothing, giving / nothing, empty, and free at last"; Gene Frumkin's "Silence will come" and then Donald Finkel's *Yes, but*: "As the last syllable crept away, / he felt a peculiar light," "as if words were the burden / he'd been bearing, all his life."

Lasting is, finally, a collective coming to terms with mortality. How? One way is with humor, as with Alvin Greenberg's "this is the way it usually goes: just a little at a time, / the body's integrity peeling away like your old white ford, / losing a right side mirror, then the left quarter's chrome trim, / the antenna, the rear bumper, the passenger side door handle," as with Billy Collins' "Forgetfulness": "It is as if, one by one, the memories you used to harbor / decided to retire to the southern hemisphere of the brain, / to a little fishing village where there are no phones."

Perspective helps the coming to terms. "…For even sorrow / Seems bearable when studied at a distance," writes Dana Gioia in "The Lost Garden." Yet even as we reconcile ourselves, there's the little sweet grief of possibilities now impossible: "To know the past forever lost yet seeing / Behind the wall a garden still in blossom."

Sometimes a rebellious attitude can help. In "Götterdämmerung," Rita Dove insists: "To hell with wisdom. They're all wrong. / I'll never be through with my life."

At last, the book offers the understanding that may allow the final coming to terms, and it does it as only poets can—not settling for moans or self-pity, but taking the grim subject of the body's decline and going somewhere with it. And the somewhere is often an affirmation: Leslie Ullman pledges in "Hot Flash Continuum" "…to stay / aboard, through hell and high water, this body / so much mine, awash in its / season, open to every kiss of air." The somewhere is often a startled recognition, as in Chase Twichell's "The Ceiling": "Look at my 52-year-old legs, / starting to ache / for their last lover, the dirt."

Awareness of mortality gives us lessons, such as Stephen Dunn's: "A heart is to be spent." Awareness of mortality keeps us fully alive, such as N. Scott Momaday's injunction in "To an Aged Bear": "…Mortality / Is your shadow and your shade. / Translate yourself to spirit; / Be present on your journey."

In Louis Simpson's poem "Grand Forks," an old woman takes a course in writing: "In this place it is clear that the word / is with us, and nowhere else." In *Lasting*, the poets' words are with us, keeping us *here* while we are here.

—*Meg Files*

"the heart's tough muscle—weak still in gratitude"

—W.D. Snodgrass

Part 1:
Looking at Aging Faces

And if you look carefully, you can see,
By glimpsing us just after we wake,
Who we are.

—Robert Bly

Robert Bly

LOOKING AT AGING FACES

Some faces get older and remain who they are. Oh
You can see disappointment there, where parent-teacher
Meetings have affected the chin; or the nose got pushed
To one side by deaths. So many things happen:
People move away, or your mother becomes crazy
And bites the nurse.

Each face had a long time in the womb to decide
How much it would let worldly things affect it,
How often it would turn toward the wall or the woods,
So it didn't have to be seen, how much
It would give in, how stubbornly it would
Hold its own.

Some faces remain whole and radiant. We study them
To find a clue. Aunt Nettie said, "My father
Put on cufflinks every day." Memories like that
Help. One face, as firmly profiled as a hawk,
Used to say: "The world is fair, and if it's not,
I think it is."

For some of us, insults sink in, or the feet
Inherit two roads and lose the way; for others, cold
And hunger come. Some faces change. It's not wrong.
And if you look carefully, you can see,
By glimpsing us just after we wake,
Who we are.

Pattiann Rogers

INTO THE WIND'S CASTLE

Wind is especially partial
to the old, the dying and the dead.
It moves among them causing dry
acacia and cassie beans to speak
from their pod-paper caskets. It lifts
the sharp spines of withered
oak leaves and the bony bodies
of their sisters to the edges
of their beds then wanes, fades away
to let them lie again in stillness.

It makes skies of the dust
of the deceased. It makes ragged
moths and raveled grey petals
of airborne ashes. With autumn rain
it urges faltering grasses along
ice-edged marshes to relinquish
at last and abandon their positions.

The wind does not desert
emaciated canyons in their stone
disintegration. It returns again and again
to worn and weathered outcrops
as if rock were god to everything
that wind will never be.

The rasping breath, the halting,
failing rattle, the expiring sigh
are the sounds the wind makes
as it escapes its open cages. Creating
transfiguration simply by departure,

it forges death from life.
The faces of the oldest great-
grandparents are the ancient
designs of the wind made flesh.
Go now to a mirror as to a castle.
Enter there. Notice the structure
of the wind's ways. Let wind speak
its name with wind. Draw your fingers
along the place of the wind's ways,
as you may never touch the wind itself.

David Wagoner

FOR AN OLD WOMAN AT THE GATE

Your permission slip has been stapled, decoded, stamped,
        And handed over to the authorities,
                Some of whom scan you now
And ask you to spread your arms, expecting you to fly
        All by yourself. One wants to see the insides
                Of your shoes, your good shoes,
As if you'd been complaining. Then he tries
        To ruin the heels. One snatches your purse and stands there
                Rummaging through it, right in front of you,
Thinking you won't remember what he looks like.
        He takes your book away and shakes it
                Upside down, losing your place again.
He wants to know if you've been given a gift
        By a stranger, which was so long ago,
                It's none of his business now, not even yours.
People are watching you, being kept back
        From the scene of this accident, worried, afraid
                They might be forced to testify. Your belongings
Have all been carried off somewhere without you
        To the end of an endless belt, to be disposed of
                Or given to the poor. A woman is smiling
Into your face, urging you to get moving
        Into the lobby of the wrong hotel
                With the heat turned off. She's giving you
A piece of plastic, one of those new keys
        That never work, yet you're supposed to work it
                On the right floor, in the right hallway,
In front of perfect strangers watching you,
        Expecting you to be perfect, in the right door
                Of the right room where you can't possibly sleep.

Ron Koertge

OLD PEOPLE

Were disappearing, so the police came.

"Description of the missing person?"
"Well, he was old."
"You fit the description, so obviously
you're not missing anymore. Case closed."

More fail to show up for checkers.
Benches stood idle as ribs. A few good
sons called up. "I'm sorry to bother you,
officer, but you know how it is after your
dad's been gone six or seven months."

Two go-gettum rookies were assigned
to the case. They stood around in mufti
scaring penny ante dealers.

Then while an old guy was waiting for a light,
a Chevy van pulled up. On the green, nothing.

They followed, collared the driver beside
a warehouse, wrung the truth out of him:

He was an orphan. He'd been snatching senior
citizens off the street, then hugging and kissing
them for days. All canceled their doctors'
appointments, some ran off with each other,
a few died from happiness.

At the arraignment, thousands of old folks
surged around the courthouse. They threw

catheters, bifocals and trusses at the helmeted
cops.

"Me next, me next," they shouted so loud
and fierce that they drowned out the sirens
closing in from everywhere.

John Hollander

"...AND S. B. WHITEBAIT, WHO WAS WELL OVER SIXTY"

—from the list of those at Gatsby's

Out of the shadows made
    by privet hedges in
    the green darkness at the edge
        of the lawn stepped
    the yellow white flannels
of the old man still dressed
        for the afternoon.

    The dancers
        stuttered on Gatsby's terrace
    where there was more
light and the waiters inched their
    way though the glitter, but
        (old men have to pee
    more often) he took his
time coming out, waiting
    in the black of the bushes for a
        moment:

    "O Diddy, don't" hissed
        the silver shadow in the hedge.

And then he adjusted his
    trousers and returned to the big party.

Donald Morrill

Nightly Constitutional

At the Road Inn in Melbourne, Florida,
the northern old emerge from their rooms
to circumambulate the parking lot at evening.
In twos and threes, sometimes solitary,
sometimes exercising their capacity for news,
they drift outward to the perimeter of pavement,
strolling clockwise through the empty spaces.
What do they see, pausing to note weeds beyond?—
miles from a beach, from children's children
whose drawings decorate their poolside windows.
Surely they've heard the chewing sound in leaves underfoot
and point to something else besides those orange trees,
the windfalls, another lug of suns.
Surely they know the life bending not to break?
Others can afford a better view, perhaps.
These promenade this edge until the dogwood blooms,
until surf shops and balconies teem with northern young—
these with fallen branches lodged in other branches,
flourishing in their one season.

Norman Dubie

THE MANDALA KEEPER

The broken chalk of lightning
across the thrashing trees
makes a saliva of the rain
flung to the streets.
All he can think of in a suddenly blackened room
is the ethyl spirits
of radishes cracking between his teeth,
the louver of tongue finding in its acid
a silver foil that's falling
past the gullet to his stomach.

The downed power lines snake
through the sump bubble of a suburban lawn
with the bloodied pedigree of hairline
on some Naga queen who loathes
the hearts of children
even in her easy sleep
near the bottom of a poisoned pond.

The rain calls, seems to have made a mistake
at the window.
A truck is approaching through the hill mud...

His daughters are gone to a neighboring state,
the yellow dog is dead of diabetes,
his wife in a wild burl of linen
is not awake with the storm
but with a new husband
who snores with almost
cardiac intermissions which she counts...

The keeper of the simple fears of people
in his room also counts
the many eighth miles of silence
between lightning and its thunder—
he knows the distant autumn storm has turned
out by the cold harbor, is passing
back through itself
like young sleepers who begin to touch:

her long hair in his mouth, her rose thumb
crossing his white stomach;
they wake to a dream they believed
they were falling from…

the keeper, who invented their slumber,
wishes for them
the long fragrance of summer days,
more love,
and all the splendid expected human plunder
of this age, no different than any other.

David Citino

A BRIEF HISTORY OF FATHERS

Do we miss a thing we love
less if, in going away from us,
it grows beautiful? It rained

all weekend, and the leaves
this morning are going
from brown and tan to crimson.

The splendor flaming from
these trees compensates us,
nearly, for what autumn takes

leaf by leaf, the lined white face
of a father growing noble
the angrier, more confused

he grows, rain like angry bees,
his empty eyes, a cold wind
coming on like dementia.

Donald Finkel

LEAVINGS

1

Tied in her iron crib like a withered baby,
sinking through infancy as if
she would come unborn, Mother shakes
the i.v. clip in her fist like a tinker toy
and thrashes at her bandages, revealing
one livid thigh. From this I came.

2

With a ghost cough and a throaty rattle,
to the twitching bluegreen star
on the monitor screen, to the gasp and sigh
of the breathing machine, her blue lips flutter,
her fitful ember breasts the dark.
Bile streams from her nostril into a beaker.
To this return.

3

Last spring she tried to leave
through the rest home window. *Some rest*, she wheezed,
and hailed a patrol car: *Take me to the Hilton, cabby.*
Leaning back, she groped for her purse
and felt her heart snap open, all but empty:
one lime LifeSaver, shrouded in lint,
two lichen-green pennies to rest on her eyes.

4

There's nothing left for me now but to leave.
On the way to the elevator, history
dissolves behind me down the corridor.
Old scars and trophies, relics, pride, regret:
my losses fall away from me like fruit,
sweetening the worm's hardtack and compost tea.

Edward Hirsch

Cold Calls

If you had watched my father,
who had been peddling boxes for 50 years,
working the phones again at a common desk,

if you had listened to him sweet-talking
the newly minted Assistant Buyer at Seagrams

and swearing a little under his breath,

if you had sweated with him on the docks
of a medical supply company
and heard him boasting, as I did,
that he had to kiss some strange asses,

if you had seen him dying out there,

then you would understand why I stood
at his grave on those wintry afternoons
and stared at the bare muddy trees

and raved in silence to no one,
to his name carved into a granite slab...

Cold calls, dead accounts.

Chase Twichell

THE RANGE

The cemetery has one of the two
best views in town (the other being
the dump), built on the same
high, rocky land, the idea being
that beauty belongs to everyone.
It's why Dad called the cemetery
"the other landfill."

From up here you can see
most of the Range:
Wolf Jaws, Armstrong, Gothics, Saddleback, Basin,
and a stretch of the Ausable in late thaw,
ice breaking up, shards cast off and remarried,
the river flinching, flexing, isometric,
a granite beauty to which it is impossible
to be unfaithful. He loved it as I do,
above all other loves.

Andrea Hollander Budy

LIVING ROOM

In the cave of memory my father
crawls now, his small carbide light
fixed to his forehead, his kneepads
so worn from the journey they're barely
useful, but he adjusts them
again and again. Sometimes
he arches up, stands, reaches, measures
himself against the wayward height
of the ceiling, which in this part of the cave
is at best uneven. He often hits his head.
Other times he suddenly
stoops, winces, calls out a name,
sometimes the pet name he had
for my long-dead mother
or the name he called his own.

That's when my stepmother tries
to call him back. *Honeyman*, she says,
one hand on his cheek, the other
his shoulder, settling him
into the one chair he sometimes stays in.

There are days she discovers him
curled beneath the baby grand,
and she's learned to lie down with him.
I am here, she says, her body caved
against this man who every day
deserts her. *Bats*, he says, or maybe,
field glasses. Perhaps he's back
in France, 1944, she doesn't know.
But soon he's up again on his knees,

shushing her, checking his headlamp,
adjusting his kneepads, and she rises
to her own knees, she doesn't know
what else to do, the two of them
explorers, one whose thinning
pin of light leads them, making
their slow way through this room
named for the living.

Peter Cooley

MAY 7, 2001

After my father died, desire died in me.
My body walked beside me, a companion,
no, a shadow; no, a friend I had outgrown
and wished to consign to rooms of childhood,
both of us skidding our trucks across the floor.
My wife sleeping beside me—I could touch her,
taking in the scent of woman, that musk of cunt,
enough to drive me wild years, oh even last year!
and feel beneath my fingers her skin in a glass case,
I ran my fingers on my reflection there. He stared back, disappeared.
Woman on the street: designs in a tableau:
circle, square, triangle, I took them in, no more to me
than offices I passed, crammed with others' swarming lives.
I was the glass man: light passed through me, light passed me by.

Sandra M. Gilbert

A Sundowner

"A Sundowner"

is what the doctor said
my 97-year-old mother
screaming and cursing

and kicking suffered
two days ago in the hospital
where she was taken after

falling and breaking
two ribs in the bathroom
of the "assisted living facility"

that I forced her into
just last summer
once she started fighting

with her imaginary "visitors,"
the "co-tenants," so she claimed,
who maybe came because she'd lived

so long with shadow in that sad, gray-
shadowed rent-controlled New York
apartment that the shadows

thickened into flesh,
became women cooking at a magic
stove behind the bookcase,

mothers nursing babies under my dead
father's desk, lovers coupling
in a secret shade

beneath the rose-silk-covered *pouf*
my parents bought before
they even dreamed of me:

and when it's dark, the doctor
said, "old folks in every ward
get stressed, confused and scared,

disoriented, this is very common"—
as common as not wanting
other urgent lovers

under her rose-silk *pouf*, as common as
saying, pleadingly,
the way she did in "assisted living,"

just a day or two
before her fall, before
her sundown in the hospital,

"Listen, Sandra,
I'm still too young
to be shelved like this."

Michael S. Harper

HEADSET (IN MEMORY OF MY MOTHER)

Rachmaninoff's Second is upon me;
I conjure all the opera music you knew,

how lush your contralto heart, how fine your gloss
of Kansas City piano music; how swift your frock

at the Comus; I watch you cutting papa's
hair; there ain't no hair like his under those deft fingers.

"Write nothing down," you said;
no notes fine enough, not even ashes.

Andrea Hollander Budy

IN THE SIXTH YEAR OF MY FATHER'S ILLNESS

I wonder if he remembers the jay
that flew into the living room window

that first day he introduced himself
to the neighbor he'd known forty years.

It lay upon the crushed
pine bark we spread the previous May

around the roses where the roots were smooth
and thornless, that jay so blue and *too beautiful*

to move, he said. And it stayed beautiful
even as the ants paraded in and out of its head,

removing little bits to their underground country.
Afterwards its body lay still

and still beautiful, as if death had not yet
occurred to it, its feathers

blue as the sky it once knew so well,
that sky it mistook

for the real thing. Some truths
we cannot learn. Some we forget,

as my father did, who yesterday
introduced himself to me.

Al Zolynas

MY FATHER, AT THE AGE OF EIGHTY-THREE, SHOWS UP AT THE FAMILY REUNION, SPORTING AN AMAZING BEARD

—For Kostas Zolynas (In Memoriam, 1913-2004)

According to our mother
he looks like Santa Claus, but to me
he's more like a retired admiral, trailing
years of high-seas glories, or maybe
more like Poseidon himself,
lord of seas and waves,
the hidden depths of shade
and swaying seaweed
and bending light.

Is this the man
who brought me a single sweet
Jaw Breaker
each day after work?
Who during the sun-drenched
summers of my boyhood
hand-clippered my hair down
to my burnt scalp?
Who lost sleep over my adolescent
forays into the *wild* city night?

Now he looks like his own father,
that spade-bearded man
in the yellowing black and white
snapshot on my wall,
a farmer awkward in his Sunday suit,

a nineteenth-century man,
a fiddle player and story teller,
old in the modern world
having outlived his time.

"I'm no longer fit for this planet,"
my father now says
when faced with the latest
technological marvel
or some piece of outrageous daily news,
his beard lending the sentence more authority.
And, despite my computer literacy,
my knowing the difference between
a high resolution TV and low density disk,
my comfort with navigating
the World Wide Web, I feel myself edging
toward the place of his planet's discards,
that place where we look and listen and cast about us
and nothing seems familiar
but the distant call, quiet and insistent, heard
like the murmur of wind in grass
or the ocean breaking on a shore.

Chase Twichell

VERIZON

My father had been "climbing,"
so they moved him down
toward the nurses' station,
very confusing, first a new room
and now his telephone is dead.
He repeats the word *Verizon*
at the speed of a slow hammock,
while I call Repair on my cell.
This is not how it's meant to be,
the wire serpent recoiling
from him as if to strike
at his memory, his recovery,
lithe black spiral,
strong-willed, heavy dial tone
swinging upside down. Sometimes
when he pushes the luminous buttons,
a woman tells him all about *Verizon*,
using the word in many beautiful sentences,
spreading it out for him like a golf course
on which he looks forward to playing,
but sometimes he answers her rudely,
manhandling the receiver,
cursing *Verizon* and his outlaw hands.
Or he's pissed because the aide
brings him the telephone saying,
It's your daughter isn't that nice?
as if it were any business of hers.
You couldn't film this. No one
would be able to bear it,
skeletons everywhere,
riding around on silver wheels,

pure oxygen piped straight to skulls
crowned by near-colorless
chains of proteins, the hair.
I saw not just my father's
long bones, but the knowledge
they withhold from him,
catheter, sponge-bath,
titanium and steel.
Oh hell, the tea's cold.
Verizon, izon, izon, zon.
Birds of cyberspace sing in his ear,
bright notes and numbers, urging him
to *visit our web site to find out more.*

Keith Wilson

THE ARRIVAL OF MY MOTHER

—New Mexico Territory, 1906

She got off, according to her diary,
dressed in a lovely beaded gown, fresh
from Washington with sixteen trunks of ball gowns
chemises, blouses (4 Middie), shoes and assorted
lingerie. She was at that time about 25, old
for an unmarried woman. Her stiff mother was at
her side, she also wildly overdressed for New Mexico
sun and wind.

What must she have thought, seeing my uncle standing
hat in hand in the dust of that lonely train station
cracked yellow paint, faded letters of welcome
for passengers who rarely come?

The buckboard was waiting and they rode out into
the darkness of evening toward the tent and the half
built frame homestead house, wind dying as the sun
sank, birdcries stilled.

I see her now out-shooting my father and me, laughing
at our pride and embarrassment. My sister, as good a
shot, waiting her turn. Or that picture of her
on horseback, in Eastern riding clothes beside the Pecos.
A picnic when I was small and how my father lifted me up
to her and she carefully walked the horse around rock
and sand.

I suppose she finally arrived in New Mexico
in the April of one year when my sister and I sat beside

a rented bed, each holding one of her hands and watched
her eyes go childlike, unmasked as a kachina
entering the final kiva of this Dance. The graceful
the slim laughing woman of my childhood. The old mother
heavy with years slipped away and the woods of New
England dimmed as these dry hills ripened and caught
her last breath, drums, drums should have sounded
for the arrival of my mother.

Thomas R. Smith

Daffodils for Aunt Vic

—In Memoriam

Your birthday in the hospital. We bear
daffodils purchased at the gift shop.

Near the ancestors, not expecting us,
you glance up—"Is it you?"—above

the pale gown not your face but
the face of my grandmother, dead

three decades. Your eyes still dark with
the pain of the heart attack, your white

hair brushed back straight, you say,
"I want to live ten more years. Then

I'll be ninety-three and you can come
to my funeral!" Last summer,

asked by a granddaughter to accompany
her by bus to Ohio, you remarked,

"I can only wear myself out once,
so it might as well be for you."

I study your hands, so open
from habit, a purse wrinkled with all

its giving, and think of the brushwood
in Boncho's haiku, that goes on budding,

though cut, because it's springtime,
and of how the body, even worn out,

its husband gone before it, children
dispersed, can go on loving the world,

still giving as the cut yellow daffodils
give their light to the dead and the living.

William Pitt Root

THE END OF WINTER IN AN OLD NEIGHBORHOOD

—for Sena

1

Today is not quite spring
but now the Marchlit windows
widen,
   show the screen
of thin dry twigs that flinch
as sparrows hop.

   Cracking buds
perch
like beetles split
      for flight:
         Gables jut,
            bay windows
          belly out against the wind.

2

Today from Minnesota came a letter
from grandmother:

  Bright storms raged around us
but they missed us and we have
         a lovely Sunday morning
nice and cool
     though saddened by the stroke a patient had
Last night she lost her voice and cannot move
her eyes

My boy you'd see my second childhood
if you could see me now   I crawl along in bed
quite on my own
           and in my infant fashion am quite free
      I feel
so free
   after these months stiffened in
traction and ridiculous in casts

We even have some fun
      The wind changes direction
often so the nurses run   opening and closing
windows   asking how we feel   too warm   too cool
                          Too late
to write much more now
I must nap

   And now we've had our evening meal
One hears the cart that clatters like so many bones
   and pauses
         and the opening and closing
of the doors to all the rooms as it passes   stops in silence
starts moving room by room along the hall
                     At the end
              it waits for us
to finish
      then the clatter once again
of glass on hard white steel

      They say my bones are hardening again
Like sponge they were   So soft I couldn't stand
                        They wouldn't
hold my body up   I weigh just ninety-five now like I did when
I was twenty and all day long
                 I wear a nightie   this one or
another but they're laundered here so often that they fade

bleached without light
  and how I miss the color
   of my hair
   "Scarlet mane" your mother called it
   and your father "Burning bush"
So short now   They keep it
cut so short

  It's good to be in bed
with the moonlight on the snow
      Two pillows prop my head
and the snow is like a sheet that wraps the world   The room
is rather dim   The other patients sleep
        and I must close
or I will wake and think this letter was a dream
  and write again and say this all again
   but I can feel our winter's
      nearly over

3

A green vine flares along the twigs
  steady on its amber claws
        and as the branches heave
   the hooktips catch:
      it rides.
      The seasons
      tremble everywhere.

Gina Franco

THE KEEPSAKE STORM

Keep

Alaska, late summer, *an octopus*
among the rocks, you write, its tentacles swaying
in the current near the skiff. Dead,
and in death, a gray suddenness
taking form, its unseeing arms cast into the untroubled movement
of your statement, where the depths threaten
but on no account surface:
ugly, like a plastic bag, nothing more to see, we got underway.

There are lapses in your wake, and even
so, momentum. I've strapped you
into the wheelchair. Hip surgery, morphine nights, the necessary
bedpan, you forget, and in forgetting, heave
at the belt with memory moving
only in the current, all arms suddenly roused. I'm off for a walk,
you say at breakfast, lifting your plate,
authorial yet,

as the woman who piloted her boat
one night through tall reefs
looming from beneath,
leadline, phosphorescent light, peering, channeling towards
the land mass merging with the darkness of sky and sea,

expertly,

and I'd like to talk to the management
this minute, you say,

anticipating highballs
of glacier ice, sweet, crystalline, fished from the bay,

but I am the management. This is who we are
together: you, counting tiles with your one
good eye, eyeing me as you labor
against referring to me to know who you are, and I,
with a knife and plastic bag
smashing two slugs of Valium into your ice cream
as if to brush these things aside, even mournfully,

in service to you, altogether too much
a prosthetic operation, the glove of the octopus
having fathomed how it wandered off point
onto shore, where you brought it, shifting
with forgetting and stillness, into being.

Rosellen Brown

THE TWO OF THEM APPROACH...

The two of them approach, so slow
you almost fall asleep between the raising
of the walker and the lowering,
the raising and lowering, the jangle like a pocketful of keys
and the steady ka-chunk of the metal cage, its meek monster footstep.
But it keeps on coming. Age
and her daughter are squeezing the bread,
bagging Golden Delicious, discussing the roast. Amiable.
Patience rises from their skins like a perfume. I watch them coming,

going, I, Cora, whose impatience, today, rises like a stench
in my own nostrils. Tender the way their necks are identical, bent
at the same blunt angle, over the cod on sale—
the mother, Annie Lofts, and the daughter,
my old friend Tara.
Tara the daughter, this is, not Tara the lover.

But maybe loving's a habit that feeds itself, like milk
when you're nursing—don't use it,
lose it. The more the baby sucks the more
you have to give it. (The opposite of money!) And Tara's love,
Lord knows it stays
accessible. Tara in her shorts and lavender tube top, sinewy, now, as a
      chicken,
calf muscles tight over dangerous heels,
leads her nearly-transparent mother
to the checkout, smiling like a saint.
(Be fair: that's not a smile for us.)

                    Nobody ever said
virtue was consistent, did they, or could be measured

52

like the price of the hamburger in my basket. I, for instance,
a good girl, known to be
just a touch too good, or at least not loose
in the love department, suffered a little failure of that love,
a blackout, we might call it, the screws, we might say,
too tight: yelled at my mother this morning
when she said the same thing over
one time too many (a thing I didn't want to hear
even the first time).
I wish I could think of a punishment,
I keep remembering how Miss Rembar (seventh grade) truly believed

that soap in the mouth went bubbling
straight to our nasty souls. She'd go to the sink behind us
and watch while we scrubbed and rinsed and nearly wrung our teeth
as if our words were underwear. Then she hung us out to dry.

Annie Lofts clatters to the door and, arms full, Tara
turns to me and smiles: *Still here? I do this better*
than you? Fondling a cabbage, foolish,
I miss her, miss my mother—miss
myself, long gone. Her smile nearly forgives me. *Cora,*
I think it says. *Look at us, child.*
Look at the two of us! Aren't we in the soup
together?

X. J. Kennedy

LEAVE OF ABSENCE

—For an old-style instructor in composition

Now that the pear inclines its weight to fall,
The wind, persuasive in the looselimbed trees,
Meets with each traverse less and less resistance.
Now shaken from your academic bough,
You skid to earth. They call it leave of absence.

When acorn downfalls punctuate the dirt,
I hear once more at that novelette of manners
Eight times projected, seven times torn up,
Your hunt-and-peck, your cane with rubber stopper
Testing the validity of the bottom step,

And still your ballpoint spattering with commas
Drab prose of fair Iseults. Who wouldn't throw
After ten years his bottle through his pane
And skim to open air on graded wings
Each essay on the nonconformity of Thoreau

In seven paragraphs, each with topic sentence?
Cars crash through leaves—a sound like shuffled papers
Batters my sleep, routs to the wind my dreams,
While slow as frost through branches steals your hand
Scoring with red the looseleaves of the themes.

Michael Collier

THE SINGER

Soaped, dripping from ears to ankles,
scarred from throat to sternum,
like a seam fusing the earth's plates,
he stands in the locker room of the YMCA
and proclaims the weather in expletives,
scorns the bosomy widows in their flowery caps.

Dried, shaved and talc'd, he grooms
his scalp, shakes out socks and underwear,
and then like the thing he most isn't
begins to sing: not songs, not tunes,
but the here and now fragments of fragments,
the *siss* and *sizz* of dentures, the chaff

and piffle of lips that almost whistle,
his arms flapping and flicking, throat
a wattle, feet claws. And what joy
in his strut, what angry magnificence
in his cherry-headed pud, red
as a thermometer in his briary groin.

William Heyen

AMERICAN TIME

When I heard the old woman speak
of a hilltop tree remembered
from her Illinois girlhood—
a bur oak with top-heavy
lobed leaves and deep acorn cups,
maybe spared by or too big already for a farmer
working prairie into pasture
a hundred years before her—
when I heard her wonder if it lived there still,
when I heard her undersong,

I thought of that tree's limbs arching
the juncture of hill and valley,
girl and country, how the oak's
whole body sang in prairie wind,
buffalo rubbed against its roughness,
men sheltered there and then moved on
into the coming strum
of boundary- and trench-wire,
how the tree's cork coat saved it from fire,
how, when the girl climbed it,

she witnessed the changing land's center,
old woman reluctant ever
to travel back there to the tree,
before her womanhood, before the wars, still
wondering whether or not the tree lived,
as it sometimes didn't, but sometimes did,
when she swung her legs again
from a limb of the lone bur oak rooted
above the remembered valley
of American time.

Keith Wilson

THE OLD MAN AND HIS SNAKE

The two lived there, almost together;
he in the shack, the snake below under
the warped boards in the cool darkness
cut by rays of light from the lamp above.

A thick diamondback, nearly six feet long,
it moved out in moonlight to stalk rabbits
and rats. Out his window the old man pointed:
"There he goes, not enough to feed him around
here nomore. Haven't had a rat or a mouse
in near two years. *He's* the reason. Old
Snake!"

The two of them, growing old, keeping
careful distances from each other, geographies
of agreement (the old man stayed in at night,
the snake never went out in the day....)

The old man pointed to his chamberpot. "Bought
that to keep from tangling with him. Can't use
the outhouse at night. Kill him? Why the hell
do that? He's got a right to live, ain't he?
Besides, I always know he's there, down under
the boards, hear him move every once in awhile.
A man needs something to keep him company
and there's worse critters than snakes
lots worse than snakes...."

Tess Gallagher

She Wipes Out Time

—*for Georgia Marie Morris Bond*

like shaking horseflies from her white mane.
She would like to mail a postcard to
the place she was born. Not just to anyone,
but to the postmaster. "When I stopped to
see him he'd gone out into his fields.
He had forty acres," she says. "I didn't
go looking for him." I gaze across America, across
death to the postmaster, walking
his Missouri fields—wide sweep of farmland,
walnut groves, rivers and once inhabited Indian caves
gouged into hillsides I explored
as a child by horseback.

"A thousand acres," my mother says, restoring
them to herself and bequeathing them
to her children. "Your grandfather has a thousand acres."
That sentence, still a kingdom, though I know it never
belonged to anyone. The land gone,
but the words of it sustaining,
as if those acres—the slack, timbrel memory
of them—were somehow currency to feeling able
for an expanse of loss. But who needs
a thousand acres? Better to have the thought
without the bother, to walk the mind under walnut trees
on the slope behind a barn long since
fallen away—as the mind falls away—the roots
exposed so the dry tendrils of small bushes
that cling bird-footed to air
remind us that air itself is a soil
apparitional to desire.

I too want to go back. Do go,
through the long stride of her wish
to make this sign of remembrance: a postcard
to the postmaster. In my mother's memory
of home, on which I lean, the postmaster still walks
his forty acres, though I know he is
long dead. Is it cruel to tell her
and obliterate that switch-back
her yearning makes to resurrect him—who now
represents a place she can't quite reach
in her mind, except through the hyphenated corridor
of his perpetual looming up
as one broken promise?
I said I'd stop and see him…calm disappointment
in her voice. Why blot even false hope
to certify a useless truth? Any god
would let this postmaster have his saunter
in the mind-works of another. I say
nothing, let him live, beckoning to us both
across time, death and any upstart moment
that chooses her.

I am attracted to this new fold in time
by which a postmaster escapes death through having
gone for a walk. But, selfish steward
of this wild night-train of moon-blasted recognition,
I want her with me. "Mother," I ask, "when
did you last see him?" Her voice has the lilt
of truth. Memory's strange accordion crumples expertly
under the tail of the monkey: "Oh, a couple of years ago."
"Mother, it's twenty years since you were back."
Then, making her arrow sing: *"How time flies!"*

By custodial violence I yank her to my template,
offer the card she wanted to send.
She forgets what it was for, uses it all day
as a page marker in her handbook

on African violets. Later she
reads deliciously aloud: *Water them*
from the top and you'll rot the crown. Always
let them take what they need
from the bottom—her reprimand steely
with innocence, so I suspect language itself
has flown defensively from the page into her
mouth with the audacity of particulate, unquenchable
matter that is, at any moment, fully able
to restore girlish laughter
to the high veranda, the postmaster's hand
closing vast distances
to my father's courtship letters,
ten years handing them over to her—letters
from her lover, far away in the desperate burrowings
of the coal mines. And now depths darker.
Twenty years toiling under us in the black ore of absence,
as the violets drink on their sills
from little bowls of the mind.

Alison H. Deming

THE OLD MAN

—for Charlie at Halawa Falls

The old man offers to lead me
past the *heiau* to the waterfall,
a public place made private
by the new man's fence and pit bull.

You know that plant? he asks.
Ti, I answer and he laughs,
you smart fo'…
He won't say the word that means

I don't belong here, though
my knowing the plant is worth
something in both our minds.
We pluck wild mangos from the trees,

five-finger cherries. Does he know
any stories about this place?
Yes, but he won't tell them.
Scares people and they won't come.

Once on this island there were priests
so powerful they could pray
a person to death. At sixty-nine he
billygoats up rocks and hills, we stave across

the boiling stream that tugs our legs,
climb out into *noni* grove, reeking fruit
he gulps as we walk. Good for heart,
thumping scrawny chest. Are they

commercially grown, I ask. He stares
as if I'm crazy. That could never
happen. They'd all be killed or cut down.
He doesn't say by whom or what, just knows

whatever forces make such a gift
would take it away if improperly used.
After hours in the woods—bird nest
plant, he says, two people could

climb in there and make love—I wonder
what to offer him as payment
for guiding me and I realize
I have nothing he wants.

Laurence Lieberman

HOISTING JEWEL

Most officials of her ilk were feared,
or hated outright, for their finicky style of scrutinizing
  the Letter of the Law. And to be fair—all seamen
    agreed—a strong measure
of niggardliness always seemed to come with the Customs

      job detail. But vivacious Jewel was one rare
        gem (as her moniker
        foretold) in that gallery
        of mean-spirited
        Legal Robots.
      Auntie Jewel, so the dock-hands
    dubbed her, was the best-loved lady ever
      chronicled in a three-centuries-
        long annals of Salt World's
        glad heyday.
      For several decades spanning
        Turn of the Century
she was presiding Customs and Immigration Marm

    of rank, a doting Mother Superior
to the squad of transient hirelings on her Caribbean job route.
    Never once did she swindle or overcharge traders,
      even looking the other way
for the usual minor infractions of load limit rules....

      When, in her mature years, she developed a fast-
          debilitating case
        of rheumatism in her hip

& leg-joints, mainly
confining her
to the use of cane and crutches,
by turns (wheelchair coming later), the men
were chary to risk her impending
retirement. So they hired
ship architects
of State-of-the-Art rep. Cost
was no issue. Skippers
and crews, together, donated nesteggs to design

an ingenious hookup of block-and-tackle
davit rings that could be fitted to any of the standard model
Clipper Ships that frequented the salt-works.
The rig, which resembled
a mini-forklift, was quickly adaptable for transfer

from one size ship to another. After some years
of working this pulley
device, the men broke into song—
chanting honorific
verses to fit
their slapdash tunes—at the grandly
comic sight of Jewel leather-strapped & roped
to her wheelchair. She slowly cranked
upwards from dockside, then
lowered—inch
by creaky inch—through each ship's
gap in the forecastle
(a few squarish trapdoors enlarged to compensate

her bulk), and inspected the ample contents
of storage bins in the hold. Pencil and notepad in hand, Jewel
scrawled her snappy calculations, perhaps imposing
a couple of token fines—
to keep ye feckless roustabouts and sneakthieves toeing

the line. Whatever nominal charges she levied
on the skippers, great rounds
of applause greeted her wobbly chair
lofted overhead
as she rose
from the dark hold, taking a wide arc
outswung from shipside, then dangled to wharf
edge. And squeaking on her donkey cart
back to the fiscal Morse
telegraph
of her Customs House, she'd wave—
radiant with smiles—
to her good buddies lined up on ship deck bowing.

Greg Pape

ZAHKIA

—Highway City, California

Once a week Zahkia Famie made the trip
to the butcher to ask after the legs of lamb.
After inspecting what lay chilled in the case
and what the butcher lifted from its hook
in the cold box, after careful deliberations
based on several lifetimes of experience
in the markets of the middle east
and the peculiar culinary esthetic handed down
through the family for generations, after
commenting on the weather and inquiring
about the health of the butcher, his wife,
his children, she made her selection
and paid with cash. Though her tongue
was at times as sharp as her knives
she sang behind the screens of her kitchen
or beneath the olive trees as she cut
the lamb into portions and set aside the fat
for soap. What she thought about The Doors,
Purple Haze, and the young men and women
who swam naked in her water trough
only a native speaker of Syrian could say.
Matriarch of the secret gardens
on the outskirts of Highway City where
illegal soldiers of fortune slept beneath
the poisonous oleanders and whole families
came with buckets to harvest the fallen figs,
she dispensed wisdom like a turtle, grace
like a fox, and fed whoever was hungry.
I don't know if her gift was dignity or craft,

though she possessed both in abundance.
What I took from her was what I needed
most, a temporary home and that kind
of confidence the uprooted young take
from the steadfast old. She didn't seem
to notice the screaming in the orchard.
She didn't stare at the full moon
from the bottom of the water trough.
She didn't scrape the black powder
from the bullet to light the hookah
with a flash. She rose each day
at dawn and watered the tomatoes.

David Ray

CHARLOTTE THE CENTENARIAN

My neighbor did not love me.
"You're the worst man who ever
came over the mountains," she said,
"and that's a lot of bad men."

She was a hundred years old
and mad because I had parked
under a pine tree she claimed
to be hers, although it shaded
a public street and the police
whom she called only assured her
I had not committed a crime.

No matter, I had also leaned
a board up against the wall
she claimed to be hers, both
sides of it, the side in my yard,
the side in hers. It was another
chance to consult the police,
who were polite as they heard
anew of my crimes—the pine
giving its shade to my car
and the propped two by four
offending the adobe wall.

After a while—and a few more
of Charlotte's calls to the cops—
I began to be proud of being
the worst man who ever
made it over the mountains.
I think she imagined me

on horseback or perhaps
in a covered wagon with
a long flicking bullwhip
for my mules. In any case
Charlotte made me feel special
for beating the competition
and providing just in time
someone to hate before
it might have been too late.

Maurya Simon

ST. PAULA, BEFORE HER DEATH

So many of my songs are gone from me,
and even my very voice has left me now.
                              —Virgil

Yearly, the slug crisscrosses his own tearstains,
the queen bee encrypts her hive with secret chambers,
the locust grafts his song upon fleeing shadows,
the worm weans herself on wolfbane, on stardust.

I sit in the heat of my own discontent, where
only the gruff sound of his voice replenishes me.
It is never enough to love, simply to love.
Better to cleave to the silver blade, its quiver.

Better to gather a basket of roses and lilies,
ivory and purple, to fast with strangers,
to bask in the body's hungers as in sunlight.
I bear witness to myself with meditation;

as one substratum of my heart calcifies,
another layer pleasures itself with memory:
my touch a chink in his armor, his touch
frugal, but scalding, and his gaze plainsong.

I grow hoarse. My virgins pile a pyramid of
fruits before me, to tempt me again to break
my fasting. I will not. Faith is episodic
initially—but these long years it's yielded

to something else…something slowly fluid—
a liberation of the senses, an animal wisdom.

I watch my sparrow granddaughter polish the pyx,
the nape of her neck softened by cilia of down,

her open face so like my own a lifetime ago—
contemplative as well water, a rosy cameo.
Is she suited for a nun's habit? I think perhaps
her fingers are better fitted to a cithara's strings.

Yet I find such flexibility of thought in her,
and an undefiled purity that enthralls me.
Little Paula, come sit on my wrinkled knees—
teach me to be like an angel struck dumb—

(Bethlehem, Summer 403)

William Pitt Root

PASSING GO

Bowlegged behind her cane
on Market Street
in late afternoon
she waits as sure
of a streetcar
as cactus is of rain,
patchwork satchel
vivid against the dark
wedge of her coat.

Mist curls at
her swollen ankles
like a lap dog
she ignores.

As the racket pauses
she hauls herself aboard
lurches
when it starts.

*Hey lady
you didn't pay!*

She halts, spins round,
points the cane. *You men,
you're all alike—
all you want to do is fuck!*

She slips into a seat,
winks at the lady
stiffened beside her.

Whispers in her ear,
Works every time now
don't it, dear?

Pattiann Rogers

In Union: Skinny Grandfather Riding a Bicycle

1

Grandfather and bicycle move together
down the gravel road, passing through
the two dimensions of shadows and shades
melding and flickering over the single
being of their creaking, rattling motion.

In silhouette it would be impossible
to tell where the skinny old man's pipe-thin
arms actually stop and the handlebars
of the bicycle begin, both the same bent
shape and stiff intention.

The rhythmic click of his joints
as he slowly pumps the pedals matches
the click of the chain on the teeth
of the gears. Both skeletons
show their thin and bony frames.

2

His feet circling with the pedals,
the turn of the wheels and spin of the rims,
spokes flashing in streaks as they catch
the light—this is a universe of heart-centers,
hubs, covenants and revolutions proceeding on
in their ways as every universe does.

3

The bicycle seems strangely out of breath now.
The tires groan on the gravel. They hesitate,
lurch ahead. Is it the grandfather panting?
Tensions strain and gasp.

The road turns suddenly, the bicycle
swerves, they veer too far, wobble wildly
close to catapulting into the ditch. Dust
flies, grasshoppers and field birds flee
in all directions. There are jagged
cries and screechings. The elements—
grandfather, bicycle, ditch weeds, birds,
the sun's instant—are willing together
with all of their might not to spill
and break apart.

They resist the chaos, right themselves
and continue in balance. Birds, seed-filled
weeds, grasshoppers, road dust settle
back into the silent sun.

4

The bicycle, retaining in its skeleton
a dedication to motion and the maker
of motion, is propped against a tree
in the coming twilight calm. Grandfather,
hub and heart wavering and resuming
with falling weeds and fleeing birds,
rests in the circling frame of his sleep.
The ditch weeds and empty road,
the insects and field birds, infused
with the wheeling shadows and recoveries
of near catastrophes, are still in the revolving
light of the night. *We are all the souls
of one another*, proclaim the riding

stars, *and the soul of each moment*
through which together we pass.

David Wagoner

For an Old Woman Singing in the House Across the Street

Framed by the half-drawn drapes, she holds herself
    Close with her elbows, her clenched fingers
        Under her chin, eyes shut, her mouth
Open against the silence which is all
    I can catch from this distance over here
        In a listening house. She's wearing
A floor-length pale-blue terry-cloth bathrobe
    With the panache of a designer's ad, her coiffure
        A swirl of lavender toweling. She must be singing
Something unpopular, something seriously
    Heartfelt from the beginning or the end
        Of another time. Now her mouth closes
To a deeply inward smile as if she's hearing
    Applause. She blinks at it. She glances
        Left and right to take in the surprise
Of all this fuss over after all what had been
    Only an impulse, a private performance
        Impromptu. Her fingertips trace lightly
The line of her jaw and touch the arch of her throat
    And pause. Shaking her head, she turns
        And sweeps the trailing edge of her robe aside
With the practiced ease of a diva
    About to make her way into the wings
        Over the patent-leather pumps of the concertmaster
And second violinists, and she's gone
    Offstage, returning almost at once, in her arms
        A load of laundry, the blossoms of flowered prints.

X. J. Kennedy

OLD MEN PITCHING HORSESHOES

Back in a yard where ringers groove a ditch,
These four in shirtsleeves congregate to pitch
Dirt-burnished iron. With appraising eye,
One sizes up a peg, hoists and lets fly—
A clang resounds as though a smith had struck
Fire from a forge. His first blow, out of luck,
Rattles in circles. Hitching up his face,
He swings, and weight once more inhabits space,
Tumbles as gently as a new-laid egg.
Extended iron arms surround their peg
Like one come home to greet a long-lost brother.
Shouts from one outpost. Mutters from the other.

Now changing sides, each withered pitcher moves
As his considered dignity behooves
Down the worn path of earth where August flies
And sheaves of air in warm distortions rise,
To stand ground, fling, kick dust with all the force
Of shoes still hammered to a living horse.

Pattiann Rogers

WATCHING THE ANCESTRAL PRAYERS OF VENERABLE OTHERS

Lena Higgins, 92, breastless,
blind, chewing her gums by the window,
is old, but the Great Comet of 1843

is much older than that. Dry land
tortoises with the elephantine
feet are often very old, but giant

sequoias of the western Sierras
are generations older than that.
The first prayer rattle, made

on the savannah of seeds and bones
strung together, is old, but the first
winged cockroach to appear on earth

is hundreds of millions of years
older than that. A flowering plant
fossil or a mollusk fossil in limy

shale is old. Stony meteorites buried
beneath polar ice are older than that,
and death itself is very, very

ancient, but life is certainly older
than death. Shadows and silhouettes
created by primordial seastorms

erupting in crests high above
one another occurred eons ago,
but the sun and its flaring eruptions

existed long before they did. Light
from the most distant known quasar
seen at this moment tonight is old

(should light be said to exist
in time), but the moment witnessed
just previous is older than that.

The compact, pea-drop power
of the initial, beginning nothing
is surely oldest, but then the intention,

with its integrity, must have come
before and thus is obviously
older than that. Amen.

Louis Simpson

GRAND FORKS

The old woman who still
bears some strong vestiges
of former beauty, once
played Broadway in *Hello Dolly!*
and toured with a road company.

Now she lives alone. For company
she has three dogs, an unspecified
number of cats, and animals
passing through with broken limbs,
wounds, or contusions.

As there is no veterinarian
for miles, she injects them
with the necessary medication,
and binds up their wounds.

Here genocide once planted its flag,
but has been rooted out. Murder
and rape still make an appearance,
but these are isolated cases.

What is usual is silence,
or a creaking board.
The wind blows across the land
with no letup. A fence
cuts the wind, and the wind closes around it.

The old woman who lives
out here all alone,
who has seen and known so much,
is taking a course in writing.
She told me so herself.

In this place it is clear that the word
is with us, and nowhere else.

Mari Evans

THE ELDERS

With their bad feet
and their gray hair
and Amazing Grace how sweet the sound
cardboard fans
with a colored family seasonal
gift from Baker's Funeral Home
stirring heat and hallelujahs
No hiding place down here, son
I asked Jesus to change your name, child
Help me Jesus
through one more day
And, yesma'am, I don't mind working late
again and nosir, I'm feeling fine
it be a long time before you need a
younger man t'work this job
And swing low sweet chariot Lawd
somewhere there's a crown f'me
Be our heritage
            our strength
The way they moved from can to can't
preparing the way
throwing down the road
Say want you to have more'n I had child
Say be more than I am, go
Go where there aint no limits
See you standing at the top a that mountain
looking down

With their bad feet
and their gray hair
bony symbols of indomitable will

having triumphed over Goree
endured the Middle passage
survived cotton and cane
Branding iron and bull whip
crossed Deep River into Canaan
strode through dust bowl and depression
Smiled through smoking Watts and
Newark, smoldering Detroit and
locked old arms with young to sing
surely We Shall Overcome

And now
be saying Walk Together Children
we went through the undergrowth
with only cane knives and we
cut it down to size
Fight the fight, wage the wars
and win
It's in y'blood

With their bad feet
and their gray hair
they be our heritage
our strength
Torn tents pitched
at the foot of the mountain
having moved from can to can't
they be our national treasure
they be
   our priceless charge

Garrett Hongo

ELEGY, KAHUKU

—to the memory of Herbert Shigemitsu, 1943-2004

A jut of sand and grass, the northern tip of O`ahu,
The family graves of two generations,
Is where I go on pilgrimage—
Scores of unmarked plots under templegrass,
Stakes of rotting 2x4s silvering through the processionals of rain,
Slanting like monks in grey robes
Bending to kneel in homage to the brutal earth.

There were canefields all through this world once,
A sea of soft green between the emerald cliffs,
The folded rock screens of the Ko`olaus
And pitching grey seas of the Pacific.
Rough lands made rougher by profit and calculation,
Whole villages imported to work the cane,
Nineteen cents a day for a man, eleven for women,
Bango tags stamped on their lunchpails
Half-full of rice and stringy beef,
Their bodies swaddled in denim against the canedust,
Sweet muck of raw capital caked on their gloved hands.

Hore-hore bushi, they sang, work tunes about "the man,"
A Scotch-Irish foreman with a whip and a pistol,
Or a Japanese with English skills sitting on a mule,
Counting the bob-and-weave of each brown soul
Hauling its bundle of burned stalks up the ramp of the cane-car,
Chanting, bearing witness, testifying to the accomplishments of
    misery.

Gaman, they would say, "Persevere,"
And *kodomo-no-tame*, "for Posterity's sake,"
Grunting their way through resentment over the memory
Of handbills passed around the villages in Southern Japan,
Promising "Heaven" in these islands,
Hawaii as *Tengoku* of the mid-Pacific

∽

And so they came, 188 in the first ship,
Swiftly ten thousand more, then more than that,
And my ancestors from Fukuoka, the Shigemitsu, immigrated too,
In the second wave of laborers under contract—
Kanyaku-Imin, had their picture taken
Soon as they landed in Honolulu Bay
By a white man with an 8x10 who posed them on the docks.
In the photo, Toryu, my great-grandfather, sits cross-legged,
Dressed in a rough, darkcloth *kimono*,
Clutching my eldest granduncle who squirms in his grasp,
A child with his head shaven almost bald and a mole on his right
    cheek.
Toryu gazes straight into the camera with a look like Guevarra's
As his head was lifted from the Bolivian autopsy table—astonished.
Mid-twenties I would guess, his stiff, bristling hair
Is cut close against his oblong head in a Ur-, 19th century "fade."
Then, the amazing cultural touch of placing a *shamisen*,
That Japanese banjo, in Babasan's lap,
My great-grandmother off to his right.
She kneels and leans slightly into him,
Her dark face turned ¾ from the lens,
Her eyes catching the tropical light,
Some bemusement curving her lips into a smile.
U-soh—"Bullshit is all," she might have thought,
This orchestrated pose of the dandy who met them at the Honolulu
    Bridge,
Offering them a few coins, then made the exposure for this amazing
    photograph.

It's in the Smithsonian now, third item in the "A More Perfect Union"
    exhibit,
Its entryway just to starboard of Old Ironsides, part of nation-making
    too.
Its provenance is through Tsuruko, my grandmother, who got it from
    Babasan,
Then gave it to Franklin Odo, a scholar who collects these things,
Who gave it to the Bishop Museum who loaned it to the Smithsonian
    indefinitely.
I saw it first in a family album my grandmother pulled from under her
    bed
One hot afternoon in Nu`uanu, TV on to a Japanese game show,
Electric fan rattling and ringing in its cage, a mound of *somen*
    draining in the sink.

∽

It's a long way from there to 1882, even longer to D.C. and the History
    Museum.
Yet provenance is not fate, the Shigemitsus and their seven children
Fleeing in the night, *michiyuki*, led by the moon across O`ahu's North
    Shore,
Evicted from their hut on Wai`alua Plantation in 1920 during a sugar
    strike for better wages.
Tsuruko says they traipsed along the railroad tracks, hiding from
    lunas,
Stopping at fishing shrines and *lele* at sunset
To cook rice and corned beef in a bucket, sleeping on the beach sand
    and pine needles
Until they got to Kahuku and the haven of relatives
Who patched their clothes and salved their feet
And buried the youngest brother in the sandy point of the graveyard
Where most of them are now,
          laid to rest in the shadow of the smokestacks of the
    abandoned mill.

∽

Once established in Kahuku, Babasan became known
For care and success with children, "because mos' of dem survive,"
    Tsuruko said.
She was told to go along the dirt road through Walkerville
Where the whites all lived in their 2-story houses
And out almost all the way to the piggery
To the stand of ironwood trees by the red fence at the dump.
Babasan went, and a woman met her there at midnight
With a newborn wrapped in a flannel shirt. Matsuo, they called him,
"Pine Boy," a Native Hawaiian adopted by the family,
Who grew to over six feet and worked and cursed the cane with his
    Japanese brothers.

                         ∾

To get there, you get off Kam Highway and go north through the
    village
Past the stacks of the rusting mill and along a crumbling paved road
Lined with morning glories and bougainvillea,
Until you get to the 9-hole public course built right against the sea.
My Uncle Harry was once its groundskeeper, a man barely 5½ feet tall,
Who could hit a mile with a 7-iron and drop a cruising seagull
With a shot from a sand-wedge.

                              You park at the clubhouse,
Just a shack on stilts by the first hole and the Filipino graveyard,
And feel the tradewinds billowing your loose clothes.
You bow and step through the horsegate and go down a grade
Past Hole #5 and a bunker fringed with seagrapes growing out of the
    sand,
A screwpine twisting up the windblown trunk of a *hau* tree,
Seasurf cannonades sending spume and spray on the soft kisses of
    wind.

I've taken my sons there a few times now,
Taught them the bows and genuflections of worship,
The murmurs of a chant, homage to the Other Side
I brought back with me from Shokoku-ji in Kyoto.

They seem to like it when I bow, clap hands and sing,
And louder sing than the wind, knees plunged in the pokey grasses
    and sands of eternity.

I placed a cup of rice wine and a plate of *pake* cake on the grave,
Strung a wreath of purple orchids on the worn headstone of Yaeko
    Kubota,
My grandfather's sister, the last time we were there.
                            I chanted the Heart's Sutra,
"Form Is Emptiness, Emptiness Is Form," my sons holding their
    breaths,
Their postures of reverence like egrets posing in silver ponds near the
    sea.

Who comes here now?

                    Not my Auntie Ritsu, in Washington state
After 50 years of running the Kahuku 76 on Kamehameha, finishing
    out her days
In a nursing home near where her daughter lives, a letter carrier in
    Ellensberg.
Not my mother in West L.A. or Cousin Trish in Gardena by the card
    clubs.
Hardly anyone except the wind that mutters none of our names,
Except waves from the sea that pounds the breast of the earth.
Gulls cry and pipers scumble at the running tide on the sands of the
    point
Scrubbed clean of ash from the dead, traces of grief from the living
Drenched in blackened windrows ribboning against the last gold light.

                                  ❧

It is said they worshipped in the canefields at first, chanted sutras by
    starlight,
Struck wooden bells the priests brought over from Hiroshima and
    Kumamoto.

They built the temple later, on the flat parade grounds across from the
    union hall.
Nothing's left now but a chorus of stars that sing in the abandoned
    cane at night
And whatever it is that makes me go back under it, fables I half-hear,
Recoveries from a childhood sitting on the floor around the Formica
    table
In the kitchen where the grownups talk-story of time past on holidays.

"There was a *benshi* once," a story begins, and its end is in whispers,
love-making in the cane, chants of silk wrapped like silver on
    celluloid,
illicit meetings of a wife and a storekeeper, *shinju* in the sugarfields,
white chrysanthemums and broken bits of blue glass scattered with
    cremains on the sea.

∾

When *we* die, Kahuku is where we still go, no matter if the body is laid
    under palms
And a russet sky at Angelus-Rosedale on West Washington in Central
    L.A.
When my cousin Herbert died at 60 this year,
His brother Neal, at the funeral, giving the eulogy,
Spoke of our time as children gamboling amidst the cane,
Swordfights with cane tassels, screaming "The Count of Monte
    Kahuku!"
As we pursued joy through the neighborly stones of the graveyard,
Lifting piglets from the stalls of the piggery
As if they were our own desperate children rescued from the sea.

Will I go too?
              Amidst the black, spiney urchins in silver buckets
My grandfather has gathered from the crannies and stones of the
    outer reef?
In the slips of the wind between ironwood and eucalyptus
                        where Pine Boy became our foundling?

Tengoku it was called once, "The Domain of Heaven,"
And so it is whenever I say it is, sorrow like the silvered edge of a
    cloud,
Unmoored from karma, drifting on from memory to magnificence.

Maxine Kumin

THE FINAL POEM

Bread Loaf, late August, the chemistry
of a New England fall already

inviting the swamp maples to flare.
Magisterial in the white wicker rocker

Robert Frost at rest after giving
a savage reading, holding

nothing back, his rage
at dying, *not yet*, as he barged

his chair forth, then back, his *not yet*
unspoken but manifest. *Don't sit*

there mumbling in the shadows, call
yourselves poets? All

but a handful scattered. Fate
rearranged us happy few at his feet.

He rocked us until midnight. I took
away these close-lipped dicta. *Look*

up from the page. Pause between poems.
Say something about the next one.

Otherwise the audience
will coast, they can't take in

half of what you're giving them.
Reaching for the knob of his cane

he rose and flung this exit line:
Make every poem your final poem.

Robert Mezey

LAST WORDS

To John Lawrence Simpson, 1896-1969

Like men who meet
for the first time from opposite ends of the earth,
we never talked much.
You sat
at the kitchen table, in a chair
only the smallest children dared to sit in,
yelling at your sons or telling some sly story,
or silent, looking out the window,
and I sat next to you
with my hands folded,
staring at your daughter, barely listening,
a writer of books, a poet.

Now what was faithful
most of a century to the earth
and the darkness of earth
is preparing to become the earth,
and what was faithful to the light
is turning painfully into light.
Now I want to say
what I have never said.

Old man, sometimes I felt like a child
sitting next to you.
I watched your hands
that were strong and twisted as roots pulled from the earth
and the blue smoke curling upward in the silence
and felt like a child.

There were many things I did not understand.
How easily fooled I was
by your fierceness, your long silences,
your rants against communism.
How easily I assumed
your distaste for my long hair and long face
and my long history of childhood.
Still, I listened to your stories

and I remember well
the mules straining in the darkness, bitter thin air,
mountain road covered with snow, the huge logs
covered with snow,
and summer nights in the old days,
wild girls riding bareback over the foothills,
sisters of rustlers, going to a dance,
and the old Indian
hitting a big hole and going down thrashing and burning in the
gravel,
and I remember what I saw,
long after midnight in the cold shed,
the long rip in the cow's side,
the silent man with his arm
plunged in up to his shoulder, the cow's head
secured in the iron stanchions, her eyes
black and enormous with agony,
the cloud of her breath, the cloud of mine,
no sound, blood everywhere,
I remember what I saw in your eyes.

And I see
drifting through the smoke and fog
the cool sun—
through the wreckage of years, cars,
dead pigeons, dead wives,
good deals and foolish charity,
money made and lost,

made again and lost again,
a dead baby, a dead son growing rich in the east,
the leaves dying on the vine,
the dying sun,
through death and divorce and dull disaster
a young and tender spirit.

∾

The road is paved,
the hole filled in,
the girls lie under the stones
of Academy Cemetery
many years.
All the old mountain men
gone for good into the mountains,
the sound of their laughter growing very faint
and the wind keeps blowing.

Edward Hirsch

THE CHARDIN EXHIBITION

—for William Maxwell, 1908-2000

While I was studying the copper cistern
and the silver goblet, a soup tureen
with a cat stalking a partridge and hare,

you were gulping down the morning light
and moving from the bed-stand to the bureau,
from the shuttered window to the open door.

While I was taking my time over a pristine jar
of apricots and a basket of wild strawberries—
a pyramid leaning toward a faceted glass—

you were sitting at a low breakfast table
and eating a soft boiled egg—just one—
from a tiny, hesitant, glittering spoon.

While I was absorbed in a duck hanging
by one leg and a hare with a powder flask
and a game bag, which you wanted me to see,

you were lying on the living room couch
for a nap, one of your last, next to
a white porcelain vase with two carnations.

I wish I could have stood there with you
in front of Chardin's last self-portrait
exclaiming over his turban with a bow

and the red splash of his pastel crayon—
a new medium—which he used, dearest,
to defy death on a sheet of blue paper.

Sam Hamill

To Hayden Carruth on His Eightieth Birthday

Jesus, Hayden, it's hard to believe you're
eighty. When I began reading your work
forty years ago, how could I have known
that you were forty and forty is so young?
And how could I have ever guessed that I,
a young marine in Japan, might become
your student, your editor, your friend?

The way of poetry is mysterious,
indeed, as we discover each time we rise
into its occasion. And in the end,
it doesn't matter that we suffered or
did not suffer for our art, but that we
found in verse the courage to stand against
the state, political and religious.

How often you've said you don't know a thing
about Zen or the Tao, but you're a sage
all the same, and in the tradition of
Chuang Tzu and Confucius, a questioner,
a loner who has struggled to reach out.
And now to your Whitmanic beard, our bard
of existential grit, I raise my cup:

I wouldn't wish another eighty years
on anyone, but may you live a thousand,
and a thousand generations more. You
have shown me my way, and others their own.
You have praised what others scorned

and embraced essential *mu*, the emptiness of Zen.
Ten years ago, you wrote, "All old men are fools,"

and I thought, "Ryokan might have said that,
or maybe Yeats, or Ez in his old age,"
and laughed because it's true and getting truer
with the accumulation of my days.
You have no pride, and oh, how I admire that.
What does not change is change. Your way's my way.
In poetry, even the fool grows wise. Nine bows.

Paul Mariani

FEAR

—for Bill Matthews

He looked down at his desk to find it waiting there.
Fear. Blank fear emanating from the face there
on the page, as so often fear had stalked him
in the reaches of the night. True, the face was smiling.
And yet it seemed to darken the room around it.
Outside the bleak trees stood: wordless, bare, unlit.

A busy day inside. Work mounting up, small
kudos from an editor, a stubborn paragraph
reshaped to both their satisfactions, two essays read,
a letter sent, three bills paid, a student with a lame
excuse off the hook because of his largesse.
Of this and this we measure our success.

Or so he had believed. But now the gray face
of his friend kept staring up at him. A friend just younger
than himself, who now would always stay that way.
A friend he liked to think of as living on some
Tuscan mountain farm, like Horace, the acid wit half hid
by the Wild Bill mustache and the drooping lid.

For a time his friend had sung like no one else
and his friend had made him laugh.
And now his friend was dead. And if the truth
be told, his friend had written so damned well
he'd come to fear him, each squeezed-off shot a hit,
neither short nor wide. How had he done it?

Still, he counted him his friend, one who could quaff
age-old Falernian with Mingus, Martial, Bird.
Once, seated at the opera, his friend had kissed
his fingers to the staccato flight of some stout soprano
basting slowly in her painted armor. Each had shown
him how to wring a music he could call his own,

and in time the man had made himself that music. And now,
too soon, the man alas was gone. The trees stood
naked in the autumn air. The gray face only seemed
to wink at him. So there it was: his friend become
at last a book. Somewhere a fat lady began with dread
to sweat a gorgeous aria. His friend was dead.

Gina Franco

PARAFFIN DAYS

1

She prays her rosary each night twice, she
keeps track of each plastic bead, she prays
as beads slip past *our father,* past the maze
of faltering sons who visit because they see
themselves someday in beds like these. Beds she's
wet. And she's prayed her rosary away
from mourning, beads of plastic, legs of clay—
sshh. Listen: living seems connected (she
asks *who has brought this rosy potpourri*)
to voices, her voice spilling over tiles
and streets, bedroom thresholds, puddles lined
with mud: she dips child's hands into this, tells
herself the story of paraffin days:
a house, a husband, children, someday.

2

And living seems like days collected, my
brass bowl of petals, my own voice in words
across the page—yet that's gone too—I've heard
its metal gleam slip soft to silence, and I
remember this: a silver crucifix,
a pendant lost to the sea sinking that way—
it's not so difficult, is it, to say
that out there somewhere, settled in the sand, it is
still on fire, exists like a god who listens
but cannot answer except in sounds
of water, in sounds of salt crusting the rocks,
where life at once dragged up and chose its end,

its shape: the fire in the cells vivid
as wishes, as things engraved in stone, as luck.

3

This wick, lit from flames before it,
sways in the continuity of want.
As wish breeds wish and the room fills with light,
so I take hold: these days, inherently,
are mine. I kneel and watch the shadows cross
a letter someone's left to the saints. The writing
aches among the candles, desire flitting
from flame to flame, furious to realize
its transience, transcending my own
doubts. I remember my loves-me petals
all let loose on the wind, the crowned
stems left empty, but the making, hopeful.
The act itself denies any last conviction,
makes light of constellations.

David St. John

GRACE HARBOUR

As an old woman she'd spent her Easters
At the cabin by Grace Harbour
& while her children & their friends gave over
Their afternoons to alcohol & flirtations

She'd walk the narrow beach of sand
& stone & white piles of driftwood until
Bored she'd make her way up the trail
To the meadow in the hills above

& there in the bed of long grass
& cornflowers lie back with one arm
Across her eyes as the laughter of
Her children drifted up from the cabin

& she believed those days she might live
Forever even though she knew better & why

Tim Amsden

WHEN I AM OLD

I shall live in a zeppelin. You will climb the ladder
and find me in twilight, surrounded by sepia tones
and treasures: a yellowed valentine,
a mastodon tooth in a wooden box,
a gnarled walking stick.
We will look out the windows at the bewildering world below.
I will bring out my bag of bright moments,
show you bruises almost gone.

       We will linger over sips
       of old brandy. You will look at my hands,
       liver spots on bones, and think of your own
       hands which though firmly
       fleshed, are beginning to show their age.

           When you leave
           pretending many visits
           I will sigh, return everything
           to its place, untie the
           tether, and float
           away.

Maurya Simon

THEME AND VARIATION

What is dark and oblique in a face—
eclipses under the eyes, the throat's blackness
pushing up against the teeth, pupils welling
with midnight, cobwebs and crow's feet
penned deftly with thin ink, a sunken sadness
in the cheeks, brow—such things teach us
how life sweeps in, millimeter by millimeter,
into our tender disquietude of places.
Just as our breath heaves us in and out of ourselves,
just as the good muscles stretch and contract,
as the heart storms and calms itself perpetually,
so the face wears both sides, day and night,
on its skin, becomes both prison and garden.

My face nears forty now
and begins to play with new shadows.
They must crop up from beneath the light,
strange blooms that thrive blindly.
Now I approach the mirror as a confidante,
with the deliberation of a Solomon gone dim,
and the fecund look of a stagnant pond,
with an air that hangs with the weight of loss,
lifeless as a smudge of oil on parchment.
And when I question it, my mirror answers me:
Yes, childhood is just a dream your body devised.
Or, *You are a stone, a canvas, a wild*
and abandoned place without walls.

Kim Addonizio

GETTING OLDER

Sometimes what you remember is their voices again,
coming on inside you like strung lights in your blood,
certain words they'd tongue differently
from anyone else, or your own name
and its surprisingly infinite nuances.
And sometimes you remember their hands,
not touching you but draped over a steering wheel
or cupped briefly around a cigarette,
anywhere you could watch them
in their life apart from you, knowing how
they'd flutter toward you later, blind but sure,
and come to rest where you needed them.
You remember the hardness of their bellies,
the line of hair that swirls down toward
the cock, the taste of each one
that entered you and then withdrew, or lay
quietly inside a while longer before slipping
away like a girl sneaking out in the middle
of the night, high heels dangling from one hand
as her stockinged feet drew sparks from the rug.
Sometimes you wander the house all day,
the fog outside stalled at the tops
of trees, refusing to rise higher and reveal
the world you hope is still there, the one
in which you're still a woman
some beautiful man might helplessly
move toward. And you remember how one
looked at you the first time you undressed,
how another didn't mind that you cried.
Sometimes it's enough just to say
their names like a rosary, ordinary names

linked by nothing but the fact
that they belong to men who loved you. And finally
you depend on that, you pray it's enough
to last, if it has to, the rest of your life.

Tricia Cherin

ROLE MODELS

I've started to notice them lately
even though my husband's quit smoking
their instructions may be needed

I am grateful for these mentors
old women who travel in packs
what a price to pay for freedom

I do not like to sleep alone
I crave men's campfire
the proximity of bodies

when it happens to me
there will be no need to meet twice a month
I have lived in grief groups all my life

but I am grateful for the lessons
offered to me now
I am learning

even last week's widows have newly washed hair
knowing already that fresh love
is their only hope

Jefferson Carter

FOUL MOUTH

Three times since she's returned
from Boise, my wife's given me
the "look," the one that asks
what's wrong with you? I said
"dickhead" in front of her sister,
I joked about "pecker tracks"
& beside the stove I called someone
a cunt, a word I try not to use.
What's wrong with me?
                           I'm just glad
she's home. I can throw out
those self-improvement books
I buy whenever I'm alone.
I'm also preparing to tell her
about my week, how I met someone
I never want to be, an old man
with huge ankles, a racehorse owner
who called other owners "cheap fucks"
& "stupid shits," who complained
about the fucking trailer trash taking
his reserved seats, who limped over
to his cane & snarled at his seated wife,
"Help me, goddamnit! I'm
the one who's dying."

Tony Hoagland

BEHIND TIME

Behind the restaurant
the cook sits on his coffee break
in his grey t-shirt and apron
smoking a cigarette.

View of the dumpster and a fire escape
smell of disinfectant and sour milk—
yet to him it's sweet.

There's always a behind.
Behind the factory,
the pipe, like an anus
through which the poison spills into the creek.

Behind the shopping mall
there's a strip of scrawny woods,
dark and tangled like a woman's hair,
place where somebody would hide.

Behind work there's sleep and
behind restlessness,
there's a fear some people have,
perhaps, of being held—

behind people, anytime and anywhere,
there's history, and behind history,
there are the people again,

killing each other and making love;
putting a letter in an envelope,
licking the stamp.

Right now the cook behind the restaurant:
he's bald and thirty-two
his belly hangs over his belt.

He has a milk crate to sit on
He has a rectangle of sky above him
and the splash of paint high on one brick wall

He has this moment.
How private it is.
As if it held a secret.
As if it had come to visit.

Judith Minty

THE HORSE IN THE MEADOW

I saw him, that wild stallion,
when I dressed in white. He galloped
along our ridge at dusk,
ran against the sky's flame,
mane and tail streaming fine strands.

Here, he grazes in the meadow
where birds sing yellow songs,
where the wind blows in circles.
Coat damp, glistening, his flanks
burn as he paws at grass
and listens for thunder.

She is dressed in black, that old crone.
She leans on the fence, cooing,
reaches out with bony hand
and offers him sweets.
I know her. She wants to
touch those velvet ears, run hands

over that strong back, braid her fingers
in that mane. She wants to
climb on him, break him,
ride him back to her house. She
wants to hobble him, rein him.
She wants to hide him in her bed at night.

If I let her, there will be
no color from birds' mouths,
no lightning in clouds.
There will be no more girls
dreaming in sheets of fire.

Mark Jarman

SONG OF ROLAND

Roland was a Paladin of Charlemagne,
And he was my mother's cousin. The Paladin
Served Charlemange and died, blowing his horn.
The cousin spent a day with her at the fair
Over sixty years ago. The great Paladin
Enjoys an epic named after him.
The cousin is remembered as a big kid
Who never grew up. His first wife left him,
Taking only the pillows from the pool furniture.
Roland the epic hero was betrayed
By a fellow Paladin. Roland the cousin bought
A box of face powder for his younger cousin,
And on the octopus, which they had ridden
So often the owner let them ride for free,
He convinced her to open up the box.
Roland's horn resounds through ages
Of high school lit classes. There's a cloud
The carnie thinks is an explosion and stops
His ride, and banishes the powdered laughing children,
Roland, the young hero, and my mother
Creamy with dust in a new blue coat.
Roland's song comes down from the Pyrenees.
His namesake went back to school, after his wife left,
Became a mining engineer, worked in North Dakota,
Married again, learned after the death of his parents
He'd been adopted, was devastated, and died
In his late 30's of congenital heart failure. He lives on, though.
An old woman remembers that day at the fair
And as much of his life and fate as any of us
Is likely to have immortalized in song.

Marge Piercy

THE LIVED IN LOOK

My second mother-in-law had white carpeting
white sofa with blue designer touches.
Everything sparkled. Walking on the beach
I got tar on bare feet. Footprints

across that arctic expanse marred
perfection. I have never eaten
without dribbles and droplets exploding
from me like wet sparks on tablecloth

on my clothes, on the ceiling,
miraculously appearing five blocks
away as stigmata on statues. In short
a certain limited chaos exudes from

my pores. Everyone over fifty was born
to a world where ideal housewives
scrubbed floors to blinding gloss
in pearls and taffeta dresses on TV.

Women came with umbilical cords
leading to vacuum cleaners. You
plugged in a wife and she began
a wash cycle while her eyes spun.

Every three weeks we shovel out
the kitchen and bath. Spanish moss
of webs festoon our rafters. Cat hair
is the decorating theme of our couches.

Don't apologize for walls children
drew robots on, don't blush for last
month's newspapers on the coffee
table under cartons from Sunday's take out.

This is the sweet imprint of your life
and loves upon the rumpled sheets
of your days. Relax. Breathe deeply.
Mess will make us free.

Coleman Barks

No Finale

If I were dying, or if I were convinced
I were dying soon, say within a year, if
I were told so by doctors, I would write
a bunch of poems out of my nervousness
and my love for being here. They would be
what I saw on walks and times I would spend
on the phone with my granddaughter remembering
when we went to the Shrine Circus, and Julio
tried the triple and missed, and there was no
finale. They just announced—when we all
expected there to be something else, at least
a parade of clowns and elephants and jungle-ladies
riding by—"Thank you for coming, folks. Let's
hear it for the Shrine Circus!" But we have more
than memories. We have Polaroids. Briny took
them, of brightly lit jugglers and the little girl
acrobat. She'd look through the camera hole
and then look up and snap it, but when she looked
up, the camera would tilt a little down, so
we have a number of photographs of circus dirt
with part of a spotlight circle at the top.

Boyer Rickel

Two Dreams of a Son in Middle Age

1

      I'm delirious with greed
to walk among the bloody remains.
A passenger jet has just gone down,
dotting the hills behind
my father's nursing home.

      My mother and sister glide
across the lawn, upright, steady.
Their calm is astonishing—
how they resist the urge
to touch the mangled bodies.

      I fumble with my shoes
in the home's living room,
the laces crusted with snow,
my fingers cold and clumsy.

      My father's mother,
dead for years, comes and goes
through the sliding glass doors.
The disaster seems
hardly to concern her.
I can sense her impatience:
what's taking us so long?

      I help my father settle
into his new brown overcoat.
I've thought for years
I'd be good at this sort of thing.

Now that we're ready,
I'm shamed by my hesitation.

When we finally slip out together,
he begins to fade, draining away
like a photo left out too long in weather.

Soon I forget him entirely,
coming upon a survivor, a literal
walking miracle.

Ashen, in shock, his
blank expression fixed, he says
he can't figure out what's happened.
He's tired, so very tired.
All he knows is
he's got to keep going.

2

Propped on the pillows,
my father is draped
in a red plaid blanket,
hair a pureness
of feathery white,
head cocked
to the right,
folds of loose flesh
hanging from his neck,

brown and pink
moles on his cheek
and neck,
a disarray of purplish veins,
in places dense as balled roots,
or solitary
like lightning-strikes.

His lips are narrow, noncommittal,
upturned slightly at the ends,
his pale eyes faintly lit,
the irises
dark disks
of antique glass—

inquisitive and silent
like an animal, like a tortoise
stilled by fear

or fearlessness.
An essence
of innocence

arising from a body
so distilled
by eighty years of life

it has shrunk,
taking up

no space
among the blanket's folds.

As I lean closer
to this, the most beautiful man in the world,
as I lean to kiss him goodbye,

in the skin stretched
across the bones of his cheeks,
in the creases at the corners of his eyes,

I see my father's mother,
who, when she formed words
at the end of her life,

whistled almost
imperceptibly,
the extra notes like tiny

filaments
of audible light.

In my father's
whispered goodbye

I hear that song,
frail twilight breeze

over a field.

Luci Tapahonso

I Remember, She Says

"Grandma, there's a big blanket of snow here," she says excitedly.
I smile, marveling at how near voices can seem over the phone.
It doesn't seem that long ago that phone lines were finally installed
in my mother's house outside of Shiprock.
The years collapse into decades so easily now.

Chamisa talks eagerly about writing assignments and dance practice.
She dances fancy shawl; bells tinkle as she leaps and turns,
shiny fringes sway and silver designs glitter. I can imagine her
    absorbed
in the songs and drumbeats; her face damp with sweat and
    concentration.
She spent the night at her best friend Hannah's house;
they watched TV really late and read a whole Nancy Drew book!
Her 12-year-old life bubbles on and on with activity and noise.
She is so far away, and yet remains immersed in my life.
I smile and imagine her dark eyes and long, straight hair
all these miles away in Kansas.
Between Chamisa and me, are lush, rolling hills frozen in snow;
silent, glistening plains beneath the cold, still sky,
and rivers that flow in spite of the huge noisy chunks of brown ice.

But here, the evening is turning pink and two quails are sipping
    delicately
from the front pond. They lean so far forward,
for a moment it seems they will tip headfirst into the water.
I tell Chamisa, and she says, "But Grandma, if you try to help them,
they'll get scared and fly away."
I can see her little concerned frown.

The sounds of the city are distant and the warm winter air
lingers around the flat, sand-colored homes.
Inside, the scents of dinner, the tinkling of flatware and dishes
underlie the low hum of ordinary evenings.
Televisions pulsate in the background as little ones balk at their meals,
parents negotiate tomorrow's plans amidst homework reminders
and hovering overdue projects at work.
They are relieved to have made it to the day's end.
They know that night's dark rooms hold
unforeseeable dreams and tender, delicious sleep.

Each evening, the mountains surrounding us glow gold,
then pink, then purple that deepens into soft black.
The mountains know these evenings will be only memories decades
     from now.
Memories that will bring the sudden, light ache of waiting tears
and a gentle pang to the depths of one's chest.
The mountains remember the tenderness with which they are created.
They remember the way the Holy Ones sang with such beauty
it caused them to arise out of the flat desert.

Around here, everyone tries to catch the sunset.
It is always different—streaks of bright purple, long pink luxurious
     clouds.
Magenta, fuschia, crimson, amethyst: this is where these words were
     created.
I tell Chamisa about the colors of the sky and she says,
"I remember, Grandma, when we sat on the front porch to watch the
     sun set."

I remember, she says.

Part 2:
Being Old, Still Playing

To be old successfully is to linger, picking apricots.

—Gene Frumkin

Gene Frumkin

Being Old, Still Playing

As we grow older, our hair dusty now, the force of some
essential pressure moves us to death's neighborhood
where we settle down as if to summarize a gesture
toward the pain we feel. Some turn over their will to the Lord,
a comfort like sleeping in their beds throughout
eternity, waking only to pause in their dreams, to begin them again,
with revisions, now knowing where the plot is heading,

now knowing they are almost there. Old people are funny about
dying safely, taking God to be their valet, with whatever
depth they can muster. Some, of course, claim their ground
this side of heaven and hold back as long as they can
from going on the grand tour. Some desire no help
from God. But these are few, who believe in a
transcendental essence or not even that. The old, all

of them, know that there are margins beyond which
there is no belief. I see them smiling as they sit
at their table in the shade. They are talking
and playing solitaire, each of them their own game,
wanting to group, yet fearing too much contact
might spread contagion from the others' fate.
To be old successfully is to linger, picking apricots.

Gary Soto

AFTERNOON MEMORY

Sometimes I'll look in the refrigerator
And decide that the mustard is vaguely familiar,
And that the jar of Spanish olives is new to me.
What's this gathering? The butter
And salsa, the two kinds of tortillas
And, in back, the fat-waisted Mrs. Butterworth.
I'll study the plate of cross-legged chicken,
And close the refrigerator and lean on the kitchen counter.
Is this old age? The faucet drips.
The linoleum blisters when you walk on it.
The magnets on the refrigerator crawl down
With the gravity of expired coupons and doctor bills.
Sometimes I'll roll my tongue in my mouth.
Is this thirst or desire? Is this pain
Or my foot going to sleep? I know the factory
Inside my stomach has gone quiet.
My hair falls as I stand. My lungs are bean plants
Of disappearing air. My body sends signals, like now:
A healthy fleck is floating across my vision.
I watch it cross. It's going to attack a virus
On the right side of my body
And, later, travel down my throat to take care of knee,
Little latch of hurt. I swallow three times.
I have to help my body parts. Fellas, sour liver
and trusty kidney, I'm full of hope.
I open the refrigerator.
I've seen this stuff before. What's this?
The blow dart of bran? Chinese ginger?
No, fellas, they're carrots. The orange, I hear,
Is good for your eyes.

Leslie Ullman

HOT FLASH CONTINUUM

—a deadline I've just remembered
sends sparks to neurons to fire up
all cylinders, a rush of engines
in my chest—then liftoff, streaming
vapors, distillation….It leaves me
in sweat like a layer of silk. So nature
conspires to expose the real me,
all coffee nerves and future shock,
racing the whip since birth—
now Alix is talking about narrative
strategies and I'm over my head
in hot water, treading
the un-Aristotelian rawness
of my notes, while my fingers
smear the page. Oh, for a walk-in freezer….
I would let the ice-glove tighten
around me and not mind
a hanging carcass or two, the lack
of renewable air. I would thrust
my face inches from the fan
strong enough to stir all the pages
in this room's open notebooks, and groan
with pleasure like my red horse
rolling after the saddle's lifted away.
Now it trails off like a flu….A trial
with no outcome. An itch that says
beauty will leave me with no
proof it was ever here. I can feel
my whole self crowding my
cheekbones, my face a gabled house.
Remember the midnight rain.

Remember drinking wine
and singing in the wet grass.
I'm scarcely older than I've been
but where am I going, riding
these waves that come
like inspiration? My slippery fingers
cleave to the pen: I pledge to stay
aboard, through hell
and high water, this body
so much mine, awash in its
season, open to every kiss of air.

W. S. Merwin

To My Legs

Tonight I look at you
as I never did before
and think of the old horses
the little I was told about them

out of gratitude
comes a recognition
of being too late
standing on the empty
platform in the wrong
clothes or none at all
whatever may have been said
before during or afterward

all at once the old horses
were nowhere to be seen
after they had brought us
so far without a word
and I know what happens
to them however
I may pretend not to
a last step into the air
and out of gratitude comes
a picture of nothing

the speechless
obedient journeys
the running in battles
as the fields fall silent
the full veins of youth
gone without a sound

Bernardo Taiz

SLOW SKID

At this rate I'll be able
to pick up some spending money
the next time a carny troupe
swings through the Central Coast.

I imagine myself in the same tent
with a two-headed bantam rooster,
a one-thousand-pound man with no nose,
and a guy that can down
eight hundred oysters on the half-shell
in less than a minute.

Vascular system gridlocked,
vertebrae reconfigured,
a foot of colon excised here,
a grand toe bonsai'd there,
and a middle toe lopped off
like the head of a rattler—
snake eyes, the black beads of melanoma.

This morning, I left my lower partial
sitting on the dentist's counter,
embedded, like a fossil, in a tray of algenet,
this journey a crapshoot, always of diminishing returns.

And now I'm home, a gaping
new hole in my gum and jawbone,
noting that the color of the latest prosthesis
is slightly off, trying to cauterize the wound
with a little mango salsa.

I chuckle at the thought of my toothless skull
unearthed by some eager graduate students
somewhere in a landfill off Catalina Island,
the new digs of a mega-merger
between Home Depot and Wal-Mart.

They hold it at arm's length,
as Hamlet held poor Yorick,
scratching their scientific scalps,
pondering *carnivore* or *herbivore*?
omnivore, perhaps *throughastrawivore*?
the missing link in the slow skid of civilization.

It is enough to send them
scurrying to their major professors,
"Eureka" floating from the billboard of their lips
like the old Camel's smoke-ring.

It is enough to make me realize
that each absence breaks
the continuity of all things,
and that nothing will fill the space again.

Alvin Greenberg

CAR TALK: THE 16-VALVE ENGINE, SPLUTTERING

this is the way it usually goes: just a little at a time,
the body's integrity peeling away like your old white ford,
losing a right side mirror, then the left quarter panel's chrome trim,
the antenna, the rear bumper, the passenger side door handle;
suddenly one day you're listening to the kids in the back seat
talking quietly about how they're watching the road roll by through
the rusted-out floorboards and all you've got left are these sad old syl-
labics to hold you to the road.

W. D. Snodgrass

PACEMAKER

i.

"One Snodgrass, two Snodgrass, three Snodgrass, four…"
    I took my own rollcall when I counted seconds;
"One two three, Two two three, Three…," the drum score
    Showed only long rests to the tympani's entrance.

"Oh-oh-oh leff; leff; left-oh-right-oh-leff,"
    The sergeant cadenced us footsore recruits;
The heart, poor drummer, gone lame, deaf,
    Then AWOL, gets frogmarched to the noose.

ii.

Old coots, at the Veterans', could catch breath
    If their cheeks got slapped by a nurse's aide,
Then come back to life; just so, at their birth,
    Young rumps had been tendered warm accolades.

The kick-ass rude attitude, smart-assed insult,
    The acid-fueled book review just might shock
Us back to the brawl like smelling salts,
    Might sting the lulled heart up off its blocks.

iii.

I thought I'd always choose a rubato
    Or syncopation, scorning a fixed rhythm;
        Thought my old heartthrobs could stand up to stress;

Believed one's bloodpump should skip a few beats
    If it fell into company with sleek young women;
        Believed my own bruit could beat with the best.

Wrong again, Snodgrass! This new gold gadget
    Snug as the watch on my wife's warm wrist,
        Drives my pulsetempo near twice its old pace—
Go, nonstop startwatch! Go, clockwork rabbit,
    Keep this old lame dog synchronized,
        Steady, sparked up, still in the race.

Stanley Plumly

SILENT HEART ATTACK

When silence is another kind of violence.
Like all the breath you've ever breathed
suddenly swallowed. But since it happened
over days, each night a little worse,
it lacked the drama of my father's death.
He went down, like a building, on his knees.
I sat in the dark inside the feeling
I was turning into stone, or, if I turned
around, to salt, salt-crystals diamonding
the blackouts. Silence is what you hear,
the mouth a moon of o's, black filling up
the body with its blood. I listened.
Each night, all night, my father louder.

Sam Hamill

AFTER HAN YU

Almost fifty-four,
and suddenly pills appear:
this for allergies,
and this for my bad stomach;
calcium for crumbling teeth,

a melatonin
when I can't sleep; vitamins
when I can't quite eat.
My hearing aid is a gift—
now I can listen to music,

and still remove it
when the talk grows tiresome or
I'm lost in the din.
I can't see a thing close-up
without my glasses. My back's

shot from bucking wood.
My arthritic hands are stiff.
I've a smoker's cough.
I've petrified my liver
with sake and tequila.

I need arch supports
in my shoes, and my bum knee
sometimes needs a cane.
My body's a litany
of small, nagging aches and pains.

That's the way it is—
not much good for anything,
and I'm not even
old! Thirty years ago, drunk
on the wine of the classics,

I wanted to age,
I wanted a sparse white beard
and a haggard face.
I've earned it. It's mine. So what?
Still need wood for the fireplace.

Ruth Stone

THAT'S NOT ME

I read that the left side
reveals the true self.
My true self has been
stitched to another face.
Not even my words fit.
I listen to what the
mouth is saying,
but I write in a small
notebook—
where is the body of
this person?

Every day the transit system
is a minute later.
The driver snores.
My feet move far away
in black plastic.

At night a thief enters.
Since then, the eyes in the mirror
are not mine.
Recently the nose
is unfamiliar.

Every day I am looking
for my face
among the faces that
I pass;
for my body,
a certain comfortable
size;

my voice, that even
now is not the one
that I remember.

Steve Kowit

COSMETICS DO NO GOOD

(after Vidyapati)

Cosmetics do no good:
not shadow, rouge, mascara, lipstick—
nothing helps.
However artfully I comb my hair,
embellishing my throat & wrists with jewels,
it is no use—there is no
semblance of the beautiful young girl
I was
& long for still.
My loveliness is past.
& no one could be more aware than I am
that coquettishness at this age
only renders me ridiculous.
I know it. Nonetheless,
I primp myself before the glass
like an infatuated schoolgirl
fussing over every detail,
practicing whatever subtlety
may please him.
I cannot help myself.
The God of Passion has his will of me
& I am tossed about
between humiliation & desire,
rectitude & lust,
disintegration & renewal,
ruin & salvation.

W. D. Snodgrass

LASTING

"Fish oils," my doctor snorted, "and oily fish
actually are good for you. What's actually wrong
for anyone your age are all those dishes
with thick sauce that we all longed for so long
as we were young and poor. Now, we can afford
to order such things, just not to digest them.
We read what bills we've run up in the stored
plaque and fat cells of our next stress test."

My own last test scored in the top 10 percent
of males in my age bracket. This defies
all consequence or justice—I've spent years
shackled to my desk, safe from all exercise.
My dentist, then: "Your teeth seem quite good
for someone your age—better than we'd expect
from so few checkups or cleanings. Teeth should
give you more grief repaying such neglect"—

echoing how my mother always nagged,
"brush a full 100 strokes," and would jam
cod liver oil down our throats till we'd go gagging
off to flu-filled classrooms, crammed
with vitamins and vegetables. By now,
I've outlasted both parents whose plain food
and firm ordinance must have endowed
the heart's tough muscle—weak still in gratitude.

Len Roberts

MONITORING IMPULSES

The tube jiggles each time
  I swallow,
each time I breathe, so
I try not to eat,
I try to sip the air
so the monitor won't jolt
with its green alarm,
so it won't flash that
red exclamation point
straight at my heart,
electrical impulses
running up and down
my legs, my arms,
into my eyes where streaks
of light are no longer
angels or old lovers
but a fluorescent screen
green as the clock's hands
last night when I rolled
onto the empty side
of my sleep to find
you gone again, a list
forming that promised
to go on and on like this
jagged line blips
up and down with negative
and positive charges
packed tight in cells
that make me who I am,
a man in sweat pants and
  flannel shirt

sipping coffee as though
   I wasn't,
ready for the rush of wings
with the next bite of toast.

Chase Twichell

THE CEILING

I'm conscious of my bones
where they touch the porcelain.
The tub stays cold beneath
the water's heat,
so it's the two colds that
recognize each other here
in this grotto of earthly delights,
candles enlivening
the tile overhead,
the perfumed foam
I lie beneath.

A word alighting
on the tongue-tip,
then gone again....
And my eyes are changing.
Oh, the fussing over glasses.
The mind sees its own machines
blacken and break down,
beaten back into the earth
near the railroad bed:
wire carts, sodden nests
beneath the overpass.
Who sleeps there,
among the dead umbrellas?

Uh-oh, I'm lying here glistening
and warm in the River Styx
thinking of death again,
bones in a catacomb.
A trickle keeps it hot,

but the suds are gone.
Look at my 52-year-old legs,
starting to ache
for their last lover, the dirt.

Kim Addonizio

The Work

I can't bear anymore what happens to the body,
how it begins to get ready, the skin drawing back
just slightly from the bones, the bones not
brittle yet but starting to abrade, the blood
slowing down in its thickening tunnels and sewers.
I don't want to see how the glossy hairs are leached
of their color, one strand at a time—
I think of how, after rain, ants get into the house,
how I first notice one or two veering toward
the dish sponge, then several behind the toaster
until I find a long line of them seething up
the pantry wall, pulsing on a jar lid, frantic
to get at the honey. What happens to
the sweet cave of the mouth, I don't want to see that.
Mottled roots of the cuspids exposed, the pocked
molars coming loose—lately I can't help noticing
how tired I look in the mornings, how ready
to return to the bed I've just risen from.
I make myself get dressed, I stand up and feel it
coming from beneath the earth, from the hulls
of their ribs and their weedy skulls, up through
the basement, the mildew and silverfish,
working steadily and humming, happy,
in love with its job of building an old woman.

Gary Soto

In Time

In time I'll be that old man in a white belt,
The three buttons of my Hawaiian shirt undone,
Gold jewelry jingling. I'm taking
My first salsa lesson,
My teacher padding about in kung-fu slippers.

"Relax," she tells me.
I can't do that, I think to myself.
To relax means that my face sags,
My belly spills to my knees,
My false teeth hang from my jaws like a Venus's-flytrap.

I press my hand to hers,
Salt to her salt. I look around—
Beginners asleep in the arms of their partners,
Panty hose twisted around ankles,
Polyester slacks puddled to shoes.

"Relax!" she scolds again.
My pompadour collapses,
My intestines sink even farther into a silken cavern,
And across the country, at that financial moment,
My mutual funds flatten to four percent.

I struggle with gravity, the mean stepsister of age.
And struggle with my teacher,
Who spins me away, then back into her arms—
Mambo kings in her hips,
The fire stomp of a cha-cha in her feet,
And timbales and trumpets going wild.
I can't keep up. She dips me like an ironing board,

Blood rushing to my head, scared that I'll fall
And be run over by the trample of the beat.

In time, I'll be that body near the fire exit,
The door nailed closed
And black smoke rising from a burning heart.

Bernardo Taiz

WOODPECKER

Tough as a homeboy in East LA,
he's top bird here, this Gila woodpecker,
dangling like gaudy jewelry from the lip of my feeder
and sporting a red beret. The others scatter,
their patience plucked grimly from fear.

But more than the double entendre, it was the caesura
over this rich pageant of Darwinian anarchy
that reminded me of my annual physical a month ago,
especially that awkward scene, first dramatized in *Everyman*, Act I,
when you're told to drop your pants, uh huh, chones too,
and cough to the east, then to the west,
that precise, humbling and defining moment
when you give it a cursory tug
and wish for something grander, if not astonishing, to offer.

Dr. R—a pleasant young man, overworked,
the latest trustee of my sullied health history,
and, of course, aware of the melanoma
that claimed a toe almost two decades ago—
is about to throw in a dermatological quickie,
once his inguinal probings are complete.

He sits on a stool, rubber-gloved and too close for comfort.
"How long have you had these moles?" he asks,
as I gaze out an east window and see the beginning of Time.
I shrink again. "Which moles?"
"These, on your penis," he says matter-of-factly.

This is where my bravado has always kicked into high gear.
"Jesus," I say, sucking in, pushing back the girth

to get a peek over the pantry shelf of loneliness
that separates me, of late, from the lower half of my body.
"I don't know. I haven't seen it in five years.
You're the first." The good doctor hands me a referral.

Forgodsake, Longfellow was only sixty when he died,
and, in a photograph at forty-six, looks older than the pharaohs.
I'm squinting at the eight ball of Medicare
and even after fifty years of sin—
lungs volcanic ash, my veins carne seca—
look much younger. Yet I wonder,

Was it across some short circuit early on—
during those sweet-and-sour days of pimples and hard-ons,
of pegged pants, Wildroot Cream Oil, and blue suede shoes—
that I learned to hate a scuff or a hair out of place
but never learned to love breathing?

In a child's mind, all things are possible.
I drift down the hall to the elevator
on the brief thermal of my own whistle,
then on the ground floor limp outside,
looking for a railing, a signpost, a brick wall,
something to cling to,
trying to find the vital pulse of the moment,
to hold the world together a bit longer
in whatever way I can.

Ron Koertge

55

is outside the door. For now, I am opening
gifts. Here is *Best Loved Poems.* I hold it up
to my neck like a tie and everyone laughs.

Then I read aloud. All the poems are about
Jesus and dogs. I start a little riff about how
few pets there are in the Bible:

Moses didn't have one. It's hard to picture
Herod with a kitten or Judas holding a parakeet
on his not-quite-clean finger.

My friends are drunk enough, so they laugh
then kiss me good-bye like people leaving
a sinking ship—women and children first.

Alone, I clean up a little. 55 has slipped in,
but we aren't on speaking terms yet. Still,
when I put the cake on the table and pick

at my name, it comes and looks over my shoulder.
I can feel the warmth from its little pot belly.
Its breath is sweeter than I thought it would be.

Jim Simmerman

TAKE WHAT YOU WANT BUT EAT WHAT YOU TAKE

I can't recall whether my assignment
is to say what it's like or what it means.
Either way, I know that the alignment
gets squirrelly by and by, and know that streams

flow in only one direction. Memory
gets to be like a telescope that chooses
for itself which end fits up against the eye,
blackens it sometimes (some joke!) when I use it

to spy too hard or too long on something
that's better off forgotten. For instance,
the time I told a lie that went running
tattle-tale off on its own like some fitness

freak, some Paul Revere of mendacity,
and left me cramped and huffing way behind.
There are other lucid transparencies
to lay atop that one—you know the kind—

like in the anatomical textbook
I'd hunker over in the library,
just a kiddy trying to sneak a peek
at a titty or a snatch. It was scary

how I had to work my way through the bones
and muscles, the liver and intestines:
all those parts I've lately come to know
stall out, wear down, call for the question

again and again long after the quorum's
been lost. Clearly, the body will break
your heart like kindling. Meantime, a forum
of another sort fires up, and one side takes

the position that the difference between
love and *in love* is the same as that
between *correct* and *incorrect*; and it seems
like someone, some dewy-eyed Webster type,

would compile a dictionary of
the affections, where whatever gets felt
gets alphabetized where I could look it up,
gets spelled out and defined, even gets dealt

into a pithy, illustrative phrase
I could enunciate, though the rhyme
and reason escape me. At my age—
which is the line people use to remind

me I'm somewhere in the middle of things—
things I ought to know still catch me by surprise
(pants down, day-old underwear gaping
at the crotch) like houseguests who arise

before I'm awake enough to recollect
they're there. It's like the mind plays hooky.
Sometimes my own words are weird and suspect
as something out of a fortune cookie.

It's from a Chinese smorgasbord place
in San Diego I get my motto:
take what you want but eat what you take.
It's true! They charge for the ginseng jello

uneaten on your plate, fifteen cents,
two bits for barbecue chicken feet.
(I couldn't afford my own bad taste, hence
ended up ditching them under the seat.)

What else have I ditched? (O rapid turn
in this stream of talk I didn't mean to take
so loosely rigged!) It makes the brainpan churn
like a voodoo cauldron of eyes and snakes

to think of things I might or might not have
done, things I can no longer do or undo
and—no—I won't be supping with the saved.
I've had sufficient. May I be excused

from the moderate mess I've made of my plate
if I promise to brush my teeth and floss
and gargle away the aftertaste?
Give my compliments, please, to the chef.

Although I didn't save room for dessert,
I'll palm it into my pocket, then home—

another sweetness I'll break to read: *regret,*
regret and plenty more where that came from.

Billy Collins

FORGETFULNESS

The name of the author is the first to go
followed obediently by the title, the plot,
the heartbreaking conclusion, the entire novel
which suddenly becomes one you have never read, never even heard
    of.

It is as if, one by one, the memories you used to harbor
decided to retire to the southern hemisphere of the brain,
to a little fishing village where there are no phones.

Long ago you kissed the nine Muses good-bye,
and you watched the quadratic equation pack its bag,
and even now as you memorize the order of the planets,

something else is slipping away, a state flower perhaps,
the address of an uncle, the capital of Paraguay.

Whatever it is you are struggling to remember
it is not poised on the tip of your tongue,
not even lurking in some obscure corner of your spleen.

It has floated away down a dark mythological river
whose name begins with an L as far as you can recall,
well on your own way to oblivion where you will join those
who have forgotten even how to swim and how a ride a bicycle.

No wonder you rise in the middle of the night
to look up the date of a famous battle in a book on war.
No wonder the moon in the window seems to have drifted
out of a love poem you used to know by heart.

Judy Ray

NAMING

An eighty-year-old twin
plays the naming game:
flash cards with pictures to trigger
not fantasy or foreign words
but his own lost language.
For a RHINOCEROS with lifted horn
he raises brows and smiles
in recognition. "Ah look! The bush…
that open land…the bush…."
But "Rhino" doesn't come. Words
trail away. "This is dull,"
he says, abruptly ending the game.
The other twin wants to give back
to his brother all the names
of fading faces in old photos.

My Auntie Tommy's real name
was Clara. No one called her that.
For years she called the roll
of the eager children she coached
and coaxed, children with puffed
eyes, children with no arms,
with corkscrew legs.
Then Auntie Tommy lost her name
and all of theirs. She used to sing
her way through housework
and paying the bills, until confusion
muted her and she couldn't
sit down to tea without her hat.

Perhaps *we* could start the ritual
now—name this room to give it shape:
tablecloth with grapes and berries,
paper-knife from Kashmir,
bittersweet from Kansas,
pumpkin, portrait, paintings.
If you arrive right now
I can greet you warmly.
Majestic music brims from the radio.
It takes ten minutes for the name
of Tchaikovsky to surge
through the waves. And I know
this isn't the *Pathétique*
only because I'm not about to cry.

Harvey Shapiro

LIBRARIAN

I thought I was in love with a librarian
in Lynn, Massachusetts.
She had red hair, a freckled face,
was thin. That's about all I remember
except that summer, in Cummington,
I wrote a poem for her that, surprisingly,
in view of the barrenness of the experience,
seems to have full-throated ardor, whereas
women I have explored for years
have left me with only a few anecdotes.
So this is the gift of youth, I say to myself,
of ignorance and delusion.
It is never given again.

Dana Gioia

THE LOST GARDEN

If ever we see those gardens again,
The summer will be gone—at least our summer.
Some other mockingbird will concertize
Among the mulberries, and other vines
Will climb the old brick wall to disappear.

How many footpaths crossed the old estate—
The gracious acreage of a grander age—
So many trees to kiss or argue under,
And greenery enough for any mood.
What pleasure to be sad in such surroundings.

At least in retrospect. For even sorrow
Seems bearable when studied at a distance,
And if we speak of private suffering,
The pain becomes part of a well-turned tale
Describing someone else who shares our name.

Still, thinking of you, I sometimes play a game.
What if we had walked a different path one day,
Would some small incident have nudged us elsewhere
The way a pebble tossed into a brook
Might change the course a hundred miles downstream?

The trick is making memory a blessing,
To learn by loss the cool subtraction of desire,
Of wanting nothing more than what has been,
To know the past forever lost yet seeing
Behind the wall a garden still in blossom.

Gerald Stern

SINK

You can't remember the sink you grew up with
let alone the sink of the year you were born
or the next or the next, and it is always surprising
seeing what an old sink looked like, how shallow
it was, what the spigots were like, how the legs
were merely sticks of sorts, exposed and sodden,
or starting to turn to rust at the broken edges;
and I remember how it was washing my neck
or washing my hair—when I had hair—and how I
had a small sink in one of the rooms I lived in,
though that one hung on the wall and underneath
for I was on the tenth floor or the twentieth,
colored lights went on and off, and there was
a filthy fire escape outside my window on
which I stood by climbing out and I wore
balloon-like shirts for I was completely at home then
wherever I went and I loved day and night
both in and out of my room and it was hopeless
pleasure eating at three or four in the morning and
walking afterwards to one of the bridges
so I could see the still waters before
I went upstairs again to read and sleep.

Maura Stanton

THE ART OF FRENCH COOKING

Julia Child is dead. Now younger cooks
discuss her on the evening news, admiring
her passion for teaching us all how to sauté,
baste, blanch, deglaze, poach, puree,
fold in the egg whites, unmold soufflés
add dashes of Madeira for the final fillip.
But—yes—they all agree—she was old-fashioned.
Who has the time to follow all those steps
in our millennium? Who braises turnips?
Makes their own stock? Coats beef with aspic?

I pull the two volumes off my kitchen shelf,
remembering how I once longed to own them
back in graduate school. But the Borzoi hardbacks,
evenly speckled with red or blue fleur-de-lys,
cost too much. A friend gave them to me
in Cortland, New York, my first teaching job,
and I used to pore over them on snowy nights,
dreaming of dishes I'd make when I had time
to shape a pastry crust, and enough money
for heavy saucepans, casseroles and food mills.

Sleet pinged against the windows. I'd doze off
then wake to stacks of freshman compositions,
lectures to write, piles of required reading,
and pour myself a bowl of Cheerios,
then trudge to class, returning to a TV dinner.
Now I leaf through the two unyellowed volumes
moved across the country from kitchen to kitchen.
What did I really cook out of these cookbooks?

There's a light pencil mark on the onion soup,
and a grease stain by the tarragon chicken.

But opening Volume Two, I find a wild flower
pressed between pages, the purple color
brilliant after thirty years. And here's another
yellow blossom, and on page 240
a delicate stem, the pale green leaves intact,
preserved across a recipe for *Tripe Niçoise.*
Five flowers in all, some with tiny seeds
flattened between the pages, a forgotten meadow
hidden among the bouillabaisse and quiche
that brings back no real memory, only a guess

that I must have loved the spring that cold year
and needed to keep it in my heaviest book.
But who was I back then, reading about pork,
wrapped in my fashionable rabbit skin coat?
I haven't eaten meat for twenty years,
last opened Volume One for help with broccoli.
I touch a silky leaf, wondering where I stooped
to pick this flower, and notice the recipe
for frozen chocolate mousse molded in meringues.
It's called *Le Saint-Cyr, Glacé,* and I read on

delighted and distracted by Julia's joy,
imagining how I might unmold this tall dessert
for mythical guests. Then I close the book
on both wild flowers and crème Chantilly,
putting it back on the shelf for the someone else
I'll be in ten years (if I'm still alive)
to pull down and marvel over, or better yet
for strangers at my estate sale to discover:
Look! A first edition Julia Child!
Amazing, these wildflowers—they're extinct!

Judy Ray

TIME DIVIDED

In the mathematical equation
that is your life, x will not be determined
until the end. But fractions diminish.

Friday already—where did the week go?
becomes Where did the year go? the decade?
Statistics sidewind down your street, flipping

pages of address books, leaving stars
for absent friends. When my neighbor turned
ninety-nine she said she had been feeling fine

but the extra year was a burden.
At her next birthday she claimed to be
one hundred and one, skipping the century,

though she showed me her card from the President,
which she was returning to the White House
with her "thank you" on the back, saying

"Bring the First Lady and come for a visit—
you'll always be welcome in the West."
The fraction gets yet smaller, and memory narrows.

We know the theory of halves
by which we never reach the destination.
And when x is known, it will seem to equal
an infinite candlelit row of goose eggs.

Jane Hirshfield

THE GALLOP

There are days the whole house moves at a gallop.
Bookshelves and counters, bottles of aspirin and oil,
chairs, saucepans, and towels.

I can barely encircle the neck
of a bounding pen with my fingers
before it breaks free of their notions;
open the door before the dog
of lop-eared hopes leaps through it;
pick up the paper before it goes up as kindling.

Barely eat before something snatches
the toast from my plate,
drains the last mouthfuls of coffee out of my cup.

Even these words—
before the blue ink-track has dried on the paper,
they've already been read
and agreed to or flung aside for others I don't yet know of,

and well before
I have dressed or brushed out the braid of my hair,
a woman with my own shadow
has showered and chosen her earrings, bought groceries
and fallen in love, grown tired, grown old.

Her braid in the mirror shines with new ribbons of silver,
like the mane of a heavy warhorse.
He stands in the silence as if after battle, sides heaving, spent.

Marge Piercy

DISLOCATION

It happens in an instant.
My grandma used to say
someone is walking on your grave.

It's that moment when your life
is suddenly strange to you
as someone else's coat

you have slipped on at a party
by accident, and it is far
too big or too tight for you.

Your life feels awkward, ill
fitting. You remember why you
came into this kitchen, but you

feel you don't belong here.
It scares you in a remote
numb way. You fear that you—

whatever *you* means, this mind,
this entity stuck into a name
like mercury dropped into water—

have lost the ability to enter your
self, a key that no longer works.
Perhaps you will be locked

out here forever peering in
at your body, if that self is really
what you are. If you *are* at all.

Peter Meinke

ASSISTED LIVING

Hunching at the adult center
like aluminum crickets
on the ground-floor hallway
outside the arthritic elevator
our chrome appendages clanking
and hooking each other we stuff
ourselves in the box and turn around

Language is queer: adult movies
mean fucking but adult centers
mean dying though both mean
without dignity in front of others
In the elevator our spotted hands
and heads shake like mushrooms in rain

Not one in here who hasn't had
adventure We've cried out
in bed and staggered home at midnight
sung songs and lied making
hellish mistakes and paid for them

or not: it makes small difference Life
is gravity dragging all together:
the sparkiest eye the delicate breast
the sly hand the harsh laugh....

If there were humor left in this small band
it would raise its drying voice and shout
knowing most are deaf: *Going down!*

But no one says a word so we wait
nodding fungily for someone

to press our number

Pamela Uschuk

CAREER MOVE

Dulled by office duties, the deadpan clutter
of my desk, memos with no feet for rhythm
and emails that stack up like B movie clips,
I doze like the weed-caked crocodile
offshore, watching for any slight stir
a furred foot dipped in shallows
might create. In dreams I lick
the golden stomach of the girl I was
and the long thighs of the woman I want
to be, each stretched like heat-struck dunes
heaped by wind's sunburned hands.
I leak from each bureaucratic arrow shot
into hide that thickens over my heart until
no one hears the ruined thud inside
my chest, the need raw as ore
beneath the earth's shifting crust.
Who would see me in this buzzing swamp
might fear these yellow eyes
the electric tint lemon oil. Look
closer and note how I take
lessons from a snowy egret, whose wings
benevolent as a saint's unfolding robes
reach up, then lift completely
from the rising stench of stagnant water.

Maura Stanton

ARTIFICIAL TEARS

I hold the bottle straight above my eye,
Squeezing out drops until they splash like tears
Brimming down my cheek. It's great to cry.
Few sobs have racked my chest in recent years.
So when a twig raked blood across the white
The doctor told me to keep my eye moist,
And now I remember weeping's lost delights,
The tear-streaked face, the broken, sobbing voice
Expelling misery in salt and rage
To let grief work its way free of the flesh.
They say tear-ducts dry up as the bodies age.
We must be harmed by all we don't express
Like oysters poisoned in their pearly shells
When the rusted tanker wrecks in heavy swells.

Bernardo Taiz

BALANCING ACT

I didn't know then
that all we got was a life,
that there were no guarantees.

And why should I
when I could balance a broom
on my chin or walk it

from my little finger to my thumb,
a child's perfect steps beneath that axis
defying the force of gravity?

I was reminded of this in the shower
today, when I tilted my head back
to rinse shampoo from my hair.

Eyes closed, teetering under the weight
of decades, that dizzying acceleration of age,
I realized how little time is left

in front of me and what frightening shapes
might lurk beyond the next turn.
The years shift things, as they must,

gravity leering like a gargoyle.
Thankfully, suspense dims, though
whatever order there may have been

is constantly open to revision.
Like an old tree,
its roots exposed by the elements,

we become top-heavy,
and why shouldn't we
when so much has gone straight to the heart?

Harvey Shapiro

THE OLD POET SUMS UP

Too many women,
not enough thought.

This is what the wind said to me
as I sat by myself under the pine trees:
everything you assume will happen, will happen,
and all of it will amaze you.

I thought I was shouting
but to the world
my lips were hardly moving.

My dreams begin to entertain me.
I can't anticipate where they will take me.
The wind tugs at my door.

I see I have entered Homer's poem,
sitting with the old men on the city wall,
waiting for a look at Helen.

Once I spoke about nothingness
though I had never experienced it.
Now I begin to know it
as I know my mouth, my teeth, my tongue.

Daniel Ladinsky

From Hafiz on Aging...

We are growing toward the unknown.
Such a courageous adventure is not easy for the old,
so my heart became young again, as love keeps it.

How depressing and difficult growing old can be.
But joy can be tracked through the underbrush.
Become like the old, hungry lion, encouraged
by the scent of his divine prey
drawing near.

Jane Hirshfield

THIS WAS ONCE A LOVE POEM

This was once a love poem,
before its haunches thickened, its breath grew short,
before it found itself sitting,
perplexed and a little embarrassed,
on the fender of a parked car,
while many people passed by without turning their heads.

It remembers itself dressing as if for a great engagement.
It remembers choosing these shoes,
this scarf or tie.

Once, it drank beer for breakfast,
drifted its feet
in a river side by side with the feet of another.

Once it pretended shyness, then grew truly shy,
dropping its head so the hair would fall forward,
so the eyes would not be seen.

It spoke with passion of history, of art.
It was lovely then, this poem.
Under its chin, no fold of skin softened.
Behind the knees, no pad of yellow fat.
What it knew in the morning it still believed at nightfall.
An unconjured confidence lifted its eyebrows, its cheeks.

The longing has not diminished.
Still it understands. It is time to consider a cat,
the cultivation of african violets or flowering cactus.

Yes, it decides:
many miniature cacti, in blue and red painted pots.

When it finds itself disquieted
by the pure and unfamiliar silence of its new life,
it will touch them—one, then another—
with a single finger outstretched like a tiny flame.

Edward Field

DEAD MAN WALKING

If you think it's a shock reaching thirty,
just wait till you turn eighty?
Eighty, I keep saying to myself,
I'm eighty and life's quite normal—
still walking around, still jacking off.

Of course, one spill and I could be
in the village Nursing Home that I pass every day.
We're waiting for you, the attendants' faces say,
as they enjoy their cigarettes on the sidewalk
or chat on their cell phones.
And the wrecks in wheelchairs out front
look at me grimly as I lope by, which I read as,
You think you're so smart, Pops,
you'll soon be right here, with us.

Actually, it's been months since my birthday
and I'm still taking it in,
and when the crucial event happens
I imagine it will also be awhile
before I wake up and realize where I am—
in a wheelchair, hospital bed, or coffin.

Rita Dove

GÖTTERDÄMMERUNG

A straw reed climbs the car antenna.

Beyond the tinted glass, golden waves
of grain. *Golly!* I can't help
exclaiming, and he smirks—
my born-again naturalist son
with his souped-up laptop,
dear prodigy who insists
on driving the two hours
to the jet he insists I take.
(No turboprops for this

old lady.) On good days
I feel a little meaty; on bad,
a few degrees from rancid.
(Damn knee: I used it this morning
to retrieve a spilled colander;
now every cell's blowing whistles.)

At least it's still a body.
He'd never believe it, son of mine,
but I remember what it's like
to walk the world
with no help from strangers,
not even a personal trainer
to make you feel the burn.

(Most of the time, it's flutter-heart
and Her Royal Celestial Mustache.
Most of the time I'm broth
instead of honey in the bag.)

179

So I wear cosmetics maliciously
now. And I like my bracelets,
even though they sound ridiculous,
clinking as I skulk through the mall,
store to store like some ancient
iron-clawed griffin—but I've never

stopped wanting to cross
the equator, or touch an elk's
horns, or sing *Tosca* or screw
James Dean in a field of wheat.
To hell with wisdom. They're all wrong:
I'll never be through with my life.

Stephen Dunn

AGING

I tasted and spat
as the experts did
so I could taste again.
I put my nose in. I cleansed
my palate with bread.
A friend guided me;
he thought because I drank often
I drank well.
He thought I might be looking
for subtleties, as he was.
My vocabulary was "good"
and "not so good."
Usually I was a drinker
looking for a mood.
We moved among the oak barrels
and private reserves,
the fine talk of the serious
performing their delicate
mysterious craft.
Yet about the art of aging
I found myself indifferent,
nothing to say or ask.
We went outside,
walked among the woody vines
and fleshy, often violet,
sometimes green, prodigal,
smooth-skinned grapes.
The day was beautiful.
My friend was happy, sated.
There's never enough, I thought.
There never can be enough.

Anthony Hecht

SARABANDE ON ATTAINING THE AGE OF SEVENTY-SEVEN

The harbingers are come. See, see their mark;
White is their colour, and behold my head.

Long gone the smoke-and-pepper childhood smell
Of the smoldering immolation of the year,
Left-strewn in scattered grandeur where it fell,
Golden and poxed with frost, tarnished and sere.

And I myself have whitened in the weathers
Of heaped-up Januarys as they bequeath
The annual rings and wrongs that wring my withers,
Sober my thoughts and undermine my teeth.

The dramatis personae of our lives
Dwindle and wizen; familiar boyhood shames,
The tribulations one somehow survives,
Rise smokily from propitiatory flames

Of our forgetfulness until we find
It becomes strangely easy to forgive
Even ourselves with this clouding of the mind,
This cinereous blur and smudge in which we live.

A turn, a glide, a quarter-turn and bow,
The stately dance advances; these are airs
Bone-deep and numbing as I should know by now,
Diminishing the cast, like musical chairs.

Robert McDowell

Boxes in Attic

One is always finding something one forgot.
A photograph, report cards, a letter
To someone dear, long dead; a bag
Of marbles, a nearly hairless bear,
A signed baseball, its signatures faded,
Almost invisible; a petrified stick of gum.
A play set from Louis Marx & Company;
One old shoe (where is its mate?).
Who would pack away a single shoe?
Tax returns. Paper clips. A rock collection.
Shirts and trousers, skirts and blouses
That do not fit anyone you know.
Film reels for an 8 millimeter projector
You no longer own. More photographs.
A mountain of them, and boxes of slides
In their carousels. A warped, cracked baseball bat,
Scourge of the summer of 1965. Medals
And combat boots, though
The wars are confusing, impossible to recall.
Marriage licenses, divorce decrees,
And books for every baby's first year. A tiny box
Of ribbons from the Parks and Recreation Department.
Mysterious, headless lamps. Dismembered toys.
A child's airplane rocker, its propeller missing.
The stuff revives sound when we're empty, when loneliness
Is a bigger bully than we can bear. We'll take anything
That reminds us of how beautiful they were, the times we had.

Peter Meinke

The Bookshelf

Lying flat on the floor because I'm old
and it's good for my back
counting coins of dust in the twilight
and squinting at the books huddled above me
like immigrants in ragged overcoats
guarding their family secrets
I think *You have cost me everything:*
stoopshouldered nearsighted soft and white
as a silverfish caught in the binding
of The Complete Works of Henry James
from hours days decades spent bent
over your pages when I could have been
pruning azaleas or hitting tennis balls with real people
Now I've been down so long

I'm too stiff to get up or even reach for a book

so I call for help not expecting an answer
but from the stern and shadowed shelves
Emma and Anna and all the lost inaccessible
women above me cry out with their special accents
words I understand only from their rhythm and inflection
O sorrow they say all of them over and over
Carrie and Carol and Cora and Julia *sorrow o sorrow* Catherine and
Scarlet
and Sonja and Daisy *o sorrow sorrow*
Molly *o sorrow* Wendy *sorrow* Dora Maud Helen Hester
and I like any man who has blindly loved
understand too late as unhappy endings pour down
just sentences on their weeping and guilty prisoner
pinned to the floor by threads
of vanishing light

Russell Edson

THE KNITTING

An old woman was knitting herself a pair of gloves.

She said as she stared at a distant cloud no bigger than a hand floating in her window, Here I knit
a pair of hollow hand-shapes with the very hands that will wear them...

Please have mercy, sighed her husband.

Does that give me permission to knit a pair of socks with my feet? she said.

Perhaps a brassiere with your breasts, he sighed.

—A jockstrap with your pissed-out testicles, you cranky old man! All I ask is a little mercy....

Paul Mariani

FERRY CROSSING

Beyond the granite breakers, a world of roiling
waters & raging spume & graygreen troughing
waves. Gulls hovering in the downdraft of a boiling
wake. Beneath it all, beneath the thrum of chuffing

engines, the endless wailing voices. Three days with my father, old
now, pointing out the same unvarying scenes once more
as I drove his car: those conning towers staring still into the cold
Atlantic, while the waves grind against the battered shore.

Three days. Then, his morning, north to Lewes and Cape May.
Late March, and daffodils unfurling, and snow-white
blossoms on the trembling branch, and spring still hard at bay.
And now the ferry wheezing to keep the further shore in sight.

All my life the chitter of the living has mixed together with the dead.
As now, faintly audible beneath the TV racket and video arcades—
that white cascade of noise by which our daily world is fed—
the charged static of the lost crackling as the world about me fades.

No doubt they want to tell me something they think I need
to hear, but try as I may, I cannot make what they're saying out.
Something about life, no doubt. Or about the end of life, a river feed-
ing the endless ocean, as if they knew what death was all about....

You'd think my father, at eight-five, would know more
about the final things. But if he does he isn't telling me.
Instead, he'd rather suck the last drop from the rind, poor,
dear man, in spite of his shallow breathing, bad hip, arthritic knees.

And who can blame him? All his brothers & sisters have now crossed
over to the other shore, and both his wives as well. What looms
large for him these days is the Silverado hubcap he says he lost
when the curb attacked his '87 Caddy, and which accouterment he
    assumes

(rightly) I will replace for him, since it has become the whirling
epicenter of his shrinking world. The Caddy has by now become his
    wife,
yearning each Sunday for some final spin. Meanwhile the waves keep
    hurling
against the prow, as we hold on for life, this mindless, precious life.

Marilyn Krysl

LAST WISH

> *I've grown very hairy all over my body.*
> —Yehuda Amichai

I think, therefore
I'm alone. Nor was I beside the sea, that comforting
monster. *The man I love*
loves another. So then: did I want them
destroyed? Or both to lose each other
to others? Or perhaps the health of one
should fail. Which one? I did not want them

jointly
to win the lottery. No sea, no squall, just me and a single
glass of water. I felt very sorry
for my body, its sluff and jowl, its
sprawl, all that drooping

desideratum. I sat with it. We were after all fleshy and graphic
companions. And we carped: where
was our glorious uproar?
                    Then a wind sidled in,
swept a riff of blossoms through the door
and threw down a slam of rain. *It's about*
time! I said, and this ancient one
became calm. *Let him love her,* the wind said, *let them*

be. Fine, I said, but my heart gushes on, what

will I do with it? *So let it*
gush. What's to stop you? After that air

was a boat, and I climbed in and went to
sea. What I want is to lie in hot sand beside a large and grand
ocean, holding the hand of whoever
comes: sun, sea, that hand—and if no hand,

hot sand.

Dorianne Laux

SINGING BACK THE WORLD

I don't know how it began.
The singing. Judy at the wheel
in the middle of Sentimental Journey.
The side of her face glowing.
Her full lips moving. Beyond her shoulder
the little houses sliding by.
And Geri. Her frizzy hair tumbling
in the wind wing's breeze, fumbling
with the words. All of us singing
as loud as we can. Off key.
Not even a semblance of harmony.
Driving home in a blue Comet singing
I'll Be Seeing You and Love Is a Rose.
The love songs of war. The war songs
of love. Mixing up verses, eras, words.
Songs from stupid musicals.
Coming in strong on the easy refrains.
Straining our middle-aged voices
trying to reach impossible notes,
reconstruct forgotten phrases.
Cole Porter's Anything Goes.
Shamelessly la la la-ing
whole sections. Forgetting
the rent, the kids, the men,
the other woman. The sad good-bye.
The whole of childhood. Forgetting
the lost dog. Polio. The gray planes
pregnant with bombs. Fields
of white headstones. All of it gone
as we struggle to remember
the words. One of us picking up

where the others leave off. Intent
on the song. Forgetting our bodies,
their pitiful limbs, their heaviness.
Nothing but three throats
beating back the world—Laurie's
radiation treatments. The scars
on Christina's arms. Kim's brother.
Molly's grandfather. Jane's sister.
Singing to the telephone poles
skimming by, stoplights
blooming green. The road
a glassy black river edged
with brilliant gilded weeds. The car
an immense boat cutting the air
into blue angelic plumes. Singing
Blue Moon and Paper Moon
and Mack the Knife and Nobody Knows
the Trouble I've Seen.

Steve Orlen

THE SHAPING GROUND

Outside, the snow is falling, falling.
She is reading a fat novel by the fire
And he is staring blankly into the flames
Like a man who hasn't found his feelings yet.
No unreachable itch yet,
No desire stirring in his pajama bottoms.

In her abundant novel about British country gentry life,
Foxes and hares, incest and frivolity,
The deepest winter of the 19th century, and so on,
The sexual event happens not spontaneously, but sideways,
With cunning, ambitious steps
From mansion to mansion across the countryside in snow.

In his wisdom, he knows that desire is sometimes as far away
As Wednesday is from Saturday,
As far away as Beijing from Istanbul by train,
Northwards on the old trade route through Siberia
Where cold is so cold you barely mention it,
You're only passing through.

The snow is falling like infinite particulars
Before they hit the blurring ground.
What would it take, she wonders, to get him going?
Some small act of generosity?
She takes his empty teacup down the corridor

To the sink, washes it, rinses it, dries it
Puts it in the cabinet. He makes a reasonable mistake
In idle conversation, some mis-memory

About their honeymoon in 1968,
And he apologizes, and she says, "That's okay,"
And doesn't go on to say, *Everyone makes a mistake....*

Suddenly, he looks up from the blazing fire
And says something he's never said before,
Never even thought before: "Honey," he says,
"Have you ever taken Jesus into your heart?"

And she turns down the corner of the page,
Right at the point where the shamed, repentant
Forgiven brother and sister decide
To go at it again, to repeat their error endlessly,
To sire generations of mindless blond children,
And the words are starting to burn up
On the page, right then, the wife, this prisoner
Of the common groove and the common room,

This female anima of all the moods
Of many years of marriage, she says, like the hungry drunk
To the Salvation Army chaplain,
Like the soldier crushed in honest defeat
To his enemy, she says to her husband,
Like an unhorsed rider to the horse,
Like the wise victim of a common scam,

Like the present tense to the past tense,
Like the anthem to the flagpole,
The explosion to the ammunition,
"Yes, I will take Jesus into my heart.
In my heart, there's room for everyone!"

And they both laugh, knowing that
The distance between the parlor and the bedroom
Is the distance between tragedy and comedy,
Between the words of the spell
And the magic event, miles and miles

193

Of household corridors in which whole lives
Are lived, knowing that this will be
The arduous trek between habit and passion.
Snow is falling, falling on the shaping ground.

Helen Ruth Freeman

THAT TIME OF YEAR

They met when their lives were almost done,
the time for revising, for wearing thin;
memory's gloss already dim.

No more battles, no standing firm,
the matters resolved or compromised,
they peer through the telescope's narrow end.

Autumn plays the scene with great panache;
past summer, dribbling a soupçon of spring.
Only the tenuous weather hints

at the chill ahead. Owls
hoot in the beech tree. She wants
to begin all over again.

Richard Shelton

THREE POEMS FOR A TWENTY-FIFTH ANNIVERSARY

1. Housecleaning

after returning
all the tools I borrowed
from neighbors and friends
and the books to the library

I am amazed to find
so many things around the house
like you
that really belong here

I had thought
you were on loan and overdue
the fines were mounting into millions
I could never pay them

so for twenty-five years
I looked everyone straight in the eyes
pretending you were mine
and I kept you

2. Building

you built your house
on my wavering sands

I built my house on yours
and we abide

you are afraid of water
I am afraid of winds

you hold me during hurricanes
I keep you from the tide

3. Grandfathering

it is time for grandfathering
and I don't know how
leave me alone I have served my turn
I will run away

then I see your hand
after so many years still pale
and slender as a wand
reach out to touch a child

and I hear you say
when it was time for fathering
you found the way
as you will now

Nancy Willard

MARRIAGE AMULET

You are polishing me like old wood.
At night we curl together like two rings
on a dark hand. After many nights,
the rough edges wear down.

If this is aging, it is warm as fleece.
I will gleam like ancient wood.
I will wax smooth, my crags and cowlicks
well-rubbed to show my grain.

Some sage will keep us in his hand for peace.

Rosellen Brown

ME BUTTONED...

Me buttoned into my flannel,
stretched out on a sheet of cotton candy-stripes
I've bought and washed, bleached, folded, stacked—

Marlene, Marilyn, Madonna, none of the silky sultry heroines
ever whispered, "Time to buy a new mattress, darling,
this one's gone soggy," or chased the dog off the quilt

when he's left, like a spray of pine needles after a storm,
half his spiny coat. The three delicious M's make the bed
ride soft as a boat on water. No one but a wife

worries if the springs are shot.
I know he feels it too, Fry does. He must. Thermal tights and baggy
boxer shorts heaped on the chair together—less than he hoped,

back when even a boy is a dreamer. Enough
or not enough? That, like the nap on corduroy,
seems to depend on the light. His thick back's sturdy, a tree stump

against my own, and mine is—I can't imagine. Ask him.
So many years of breathing in ragged
unison. Drifting away on a sentence. Rolling together

in that soft, deep runnel down the center of the bed.
When the thunder's bad, we still stay up like kids, singing.
I heard him laugh once in his sleep.

Is this what the light years bring?

Linda Pastan

DON'T THINK OF THIS

Don't think of this as a final meal.
Concentrate on the taste of the food,
the salad so crisp (young lettuces they say)
the wine so potent, so sure of itself in the glass,
it can make us young for this one night.
The air outside is no different
from the air the first night we met—
that stroll through autumn
when our life together was not even a wish,
much less a design, and we could still
walk away into separate lives,
like parallel universes in a science fiction story—
our children, now grown, no more than shadows
in some book, outlined but never written.
There isn't much time left;
the waiter is clearing the table
as if of the debris of years.
But there is still a bed waiting with pillows
as yielding as passing clouds,
and we can sink into their whiteness
as though an endless stream of mornings
still waited to dawn ahead of us.

Richard Shelton

THE LANGUAGE OF POSTCARDS

we are having the wonderful weather
of paradise the last days of a season
which has no beginning nor end
where if I light a cigarette
bougainvillea will suddenly
flame on every street

shadows of buildings
are fixed in their places
the sky is the famous unfinished
last work of a mad painter
the sea is so calm we forget it
and nobody swims

we are having the wonderful weather
of postcards dead birds fall at our feet
the trees tell lies windows listen
eyes all mute otherwise silence
the sound of my heart drunk again
staggering among strangers
less strange than friends

where there was never a first time
and now it is gone
what must be done will be done
but I don't' know what to do without you
I have few words no one to tell them to

we are having the wonderful summer
of winter which goes on and on
forgive me my sins known and unknown

my pain the worst of them
your pain not the least

the language of this country
is not declined
nothing belongs to anything here
and *to come back* does not mean *to return*

Nancy Mairs

THROUGH TIME

We are here still, my love, and again,
in all our various guises.

In the garden, the bean vines
wreathed around knotty poles bloomed
for the passing bees. Behind them
the gardener rising out of a tangle of squash leaves
cradled in his earth-caked arms a zucchini
big as a newborn. *But he lies in ashes*
beneath the stripling European purple beech,
flames of new growth at its every fingertip,
on the edge of the tangle of ferns
and long grasses not far from the vanished
bean poles, the absence of appletree.

Past the appletree, black tire twirling
lazily from one twisted arm, the girl
who leapt along the length of the garden
to call to dinner the boy hacking away
at grasses and ferns beyond and then,
in middle age, struggled back with gimping gait
toward their half-grown children trundling hay—
daughter steering the little tractor, son behind
at the gardener's elbow steadying the golden wagon-heap—
dissolves behind my eyes. *Turning in my wheelchair now,*
I gaze past the beech, through the ghost of the appletree,
out across the gone garden and the grasse
into all the realms forever now closed to me.

The girl once woke before dawn and tiptoed
from her own room into the next, where the boy

lay in a toss of bedding. Perched on the edge
of the narrow iron bed, she kissed him awake,
plunging into the tang of sweat and cut grass,
longing only to sleep there beside him,
but it was too soon in their story
and so she waved him off
down the dirt road, returned to her bed,
clutching his forgotten shirt, drowning in his savor,
drowsed. *Today in that room I rouse once more*
beside you (my privilege of forty years) and wait
as now I must forever for your arms to raise me,
heavy and helpless, into another day. I have gone
from lover, wife, mother of our children
to this: your millstone. Would that I could be cut loose
and we be, according to our vows, finally set free.

Dorianne Laux

GHOSTS

It's midnight and a light rain falls.
I sit on the front stoop to smoke.
Across the street a lit window, filled
with a ladder on which a young man stands.
His head dips into the frame each time
he sinks his brush in the paint.

He's painting his kitchen white, patiently
covering the faded yellow with long strokes.
He leans into his work like a lover, risks
losing his balance, returns gracefully
to the precise middle of the step to dip
and start again.

A woman appears beneath his feet, borrows
paint, takes it onto her thin brush
like a tongue. Her sweater is the color
of tender lemons. This is the beginning
of their love, bare and simple
as that wet room.

My hip aches against the damp cement,
I take it inside, punch up a pillow
for it to nest in. I'm getting too old
to sit on the porch in the rain,
to stay up all night, watch morning
rise over the rooftops.

                              Too old to dance

circles in dirty bars, a man's hands
laced at the small of my spine, pink

slingbacks hung from limp fingers. Love,
I'm too old for that, the foreign tongues
loose in my mouth, teeth that rang
my breasts by the nipples like soft bells.

I want it back. The red earrings and blue
slips. Lips alive with spit. Muscles
twisting like boatropes in a hard wind.
Bellies for pillows. Not this ache in my hip.

I want the girl who cut through blue poolrooms
of smoke and golden beers, stepping out alone
into a summer fog to stand beneath a streetlamp's
amber halo, her blue palms cupped
around the flare of a match.

She could have had so many lives. Gone off
with a boy to Arizona, lived on a ranch
under waves of carved rock, her hands turned
the color of flat red sands. Could have said
yes to a woman with fingers tapered as candles,
or a man who slept in a canvas tepee, who pulled
her down on his mattress of grass where she made
herself as empty as the gutted fire.

Oklahoma.
I could be there now, spinning corn from dry cobs,
working fat tomatoes into Mason jars.
The rain has stopped. For blocks the houses
drip like ticking clocks. I turn off lights
and feel my way to the bedroom, slip cold
toes between flowered sheets, nest my chest
into the back of a man who sleeps in fits,
his suits hung stiff in the closet, his racked
shoes tipped toward the ceiling.

This man loves me for my wit, my nerve,
for the way my long legs fall from hemmed skirts.
When he rolls his body against mine, I know
he feels someone else. There's no blame.
I love him, even as I remember a man with cane-
brown hands, palms pink as blossoms opening
over my breasts.

                                              And he holds me,
even with all those other fingers wrestling
inside me, even with all those other shoulders
wedged above his own like wings.

Sam Hamill

THE ORCHID FLOWER

Just as I wonder
whether it's going to die,
the orchid blossoms

and I can't explain why it
moves my heart, why such pleasure

comes from one small bud
on a long spindly stem, one
blood red gold flower

opening at mid-summer,
tiny, perfect in its hour.

Even to a white-
haired craggy poet, it's
purely erotic,

pistil and stamen, pollen,
dew of the world, a spoonful

of earth, and water.
Erotic because there's death
at the heart of birth,

drama in those old sunrise
prisms in wet cedar boughs,

deepest mystery
in washing evening dishes
or teasing my wife,

who grows, yes, more beautiful
because one of us will die.

Gerald Locklin

RICHARD DIEBENKORN: GIRL SMOKING

elegant legs, gracefully crossed.
not hopper's pallet, but
a diva on a divan,
knowing she's attractive
but without illusions of divinity:
thus not a prima donna.

vulnerable shoulders.
a nipple out of nowhere.
she hugs herself, supports
an elbow on a forearm.

anxiety as well as inhalation.
sophistication, but not
ellington exactly either.
the room an atmosphere of color
…and cologne?

home from the dance?
home from the date?
home from the cabaret?

a lady in waiting,
wondering if he will show?

we used to be able to feel good
about the way we smoked,
the way we looked when smoking.
it was theatre.
a lot of women that i dated
used to smoke. after sex,

a cigarette, a drink,
pleasure after pleasure,
sitting up in bed,
or at a kitchen table.
killing time until the next time.
friendly conversations,
with each other, with ourselves.

they write me sometimes,
now married with grown children,
spacious homes and gardens,
justly proud and doting husbands.

good times, they say;
we had good times.
they *were* good times.

they say, i don't know if
you will remember me.

yes, yes, i do.
now more than ever,
after thirty or more years

a sketch,
a smoky reverie of red coiffure
a femininity gone out of fashion

yes, yes, they were the best of times,
though perilous, now proved imperishable.

my god i'm glad that i have
women to remember
and that to some at least
i meant good times

Kim Addonizio

31-Year-Old Lover

When he takes off his clothes
I think of a stick of butter being unwrapped,
the milky, lubricious smoothness of it
when it's taken from the fridge still hard
the way his body is hard, the high
tight pectorals, the new dimes of the nipples pressed
into his chest, the fanning of the muscles underneath.
I look at his arms, shaped as though a knife
has slid along the curves to carve them out,
deltoids, biceps, triceps, I almost can't believe
that he is human—latissimus dorsi, hip flexors,
gluteals, gastrocnemius—he is so perfectly made.
He stands naked in my bedroom and nothing
has harmed him yet, though he is going
to be harmed. He is going to have a gut one day,
and wiry gray hairs where the soft dark filaments
flow out of him, the cream of his skin is going
to loosen and separate slowly, over a low steady flame
and he has no idea, as I had no idea,
and I am not going to speak of this to him ever,
I am going to let him stretch out on my bed
so I can take the heavy richness of him in
and in, I am going to have it back the only way I can.

W. D. Snodgrass

AN ENVOI, POST-TURP

*(After Trans-Urethral Resectioning of the Prostate,
men experience retrograde ejaculation, the semen
being passed later during urination.)*

Farewell, children of my right hand and bliss.
You'll come no more but in bright streams of piss,
Never more turn my bedroom towels stiff,
Whitewash the walls or glisten on the quiff;
Never more swim like salmon or rough Norse
Invaders swarming upstream to the source.
Once, ovaries were ovaries; sperms, sperms.
In nine short months you brought us all to terms
When captive loins were sentenced by your court
To long years, lawyers' fees and child support.
You cared for just one thing—aye, that's the rub:
Each of you, at your Health and Country Club
Timed training laps, did pushups by the pool
Shunning each voice that cried, "Back, back you fools,
We'll all be killed—it's a blow job!" You hurled
Yourselves, bluff hardy semen, on the world
Like Noah's load that crested with the Flood
To populate the land and stand at stud.
Ink of my pen, you words spent ἐν ἀρχή
This writer, knowing all he's cast away,
Knowing your creamy genes and DNA
Encodes our texts, pirates and then reprints us, says,
"Good night, bad cess to you, sweet prince and princesses."

Timothy Liu

BETWEEN YOUTH AND DEATH,

a long humiliation. Time's winged chariot

transporting Botox, Viagra and every other
blockbuster drug reminding us how flesh

hardly lasts—a widower's surreptitious leer

off-loading unmet need onto torsos gathered
in the sauna's steamy dark—such refusal

the only contact his body has had in years—

Dorianne Laux

After Twelve Days of Rain

I couldn't name it, the sweet
sadness welling up in me for weeks.
So I cleaned, found myself standing
in a room with a rag in my hand,
the birds calling time-to-go, time-to-go.
And like an old woman near the end
of her life I could hear it, the voice
of a man I never loved who pressed
my breasts to his lips and whispered
"My little doves, my white, white lilies."
I could almost cry when I remember it.

I don't remember when I began
to call everyone "sweetie,"
as if they were my daughters,
my darlings, my little birds.
I have always loved too much,
or not enough. Last night
I read a poem about God and almost
believed it—God sipping coffee,
smoking cherry tobacco. I've arrived
at a time in my life when I could believe
almost anything.

Today, pumping gas into my old car, I stood
hatless in the rain and the whole world
went silent—cars on the wet street
sliding past without sound, the attendant's
mouth opening and closing on air
as he walked from pump to pump, his footsteps
erased in the rain—nothing

but the tiny numbers in their square windows
rolling by my shoulder, the unstoppable seconds
gliding by as I stood at the Chevron,
balanced evenly on my two feet, a gas nozzle
gripped in my hand, my hair gathering rain.

And I saw it didn't matter
who had loved me or who I loved. I was alone.
The black oily asphalt, the slick beauty
of the Iranian attendant, the thickening
clouds—nothing was mine. And I understood
finally, after a semester of philosophy,
a thousand books of poetry, after death
and childbirth and the startled cries of men
who called out my name as they entered me,
I finally believed I was alone, felt it
in my actual, visceral heart, heard it echo
like a thin bell. And the sounds
came back, the slish of tires
and footsteps, all the delicate cargo
they carried saying thank you
and yes. So I paid and climbed into my car
as if nothing had happened—
as if everything mattered—What else could I do?

I drove to the grocery store
and bought wheat bread and milk,
a candy bar wrapped in gold foil,
smiled at the teenaged cashier
with the pimpled face and the plastic
name plate pinned above her small breast,
and knew her secret, her sweet fear,
Little bird. Little darling. She handed me
my change, my brown bag, a torn receipt,
pushed the cash drawer in with her hip
and smiled back.

C. K. Williams

OLD MAN

Special: Big Tits, says the advertisement for a soft-core magazine on our
      neighborhood newsstand,
but forget her breasts—a lush, fresh-lipped blonde, skin glowing gold,
      sprawls there, resplendent.
Sixty nearly, yet these hardly tangible, hardly better than harlots can still
      stir me.

Maybe coming of age in the American sensual darkness, never seeing
      an unsmudged nipple,
an uncensored vagina, has left me forever infected with an unquench-
      able lust of the eye:
always that erotic murmur—I'm hardly myself if I'm not in a state of
      incipient desire.

God knows, though, there are worse twists your obsessions can take: last
      year, in Israel,
a young ultra-Orthodox rabbi, guiding some teen-aged girls through the
      shrine of the *Shoah,*
forbade them to look in one room because there were images in it he
      said were licentious.

The display was a photo: men and women, stripped naked, some trying
      to cover their genitals,
others too frightened to bother, lined up in snow waiting to be shot and
      thrown in a ditch.
The girls to my horror averted their gaze: what carnal mistrust had their
      teacher taught them?

Even that, though…Another confession: once, in a book on pre-war
      Poland, a studio-portrait,

an absolute angel, with tormented, tormenting eyes; I kept finding myself at her page;
that she died in the camps made her, I didn't dare wonder why, more
present, more precious.

"Died in the camps": that, too, people, or Jews anyway, kept from their
children back then,
but it was like sex, you didn't have to be told. Sex and death: how close
they can seem.
So constantly conscious now of death moving towards me, sometimes I
think I confound them.

My wife's loveliness almost consumes me, my passion for her goes beyond reasonable bounds;
when we make love, her holding me, everywhere all around me, I'm
there and not there,
my mind teems, jumbles of faces, voices, impressions: I live my life over
as though I were drowning.

…Then I am drowning, in despair, at having to leave her, this, everything, all: unbearable, awful…
Still, to be able to die with no special contrition, not having been slaugh-
tered or enslaved,
and not having to know history's next mad rage or regression—it might
be a relief.

No, again no, I don't mean that for a moment, what I mean is the world
holds me so tightly,
the good and the bad, my own follies and weakness, that even this
counterfeit Venus,
with her sham heat and her bosom probably plumped with gel, so moves
me my breath catches.

Vamp, siren, seductress, how much more she reveals in her glare of ink
than she knows;
how she incarnates our desperate human need for regard, our passion
to live in beauty,

to be beauty, to be cherished, by glances if by no more, of something
  like love, or love.

Greg Pape

MORPHINE

On the table as morphine dripped
in the I.V., before he floated away
beyond care, he watched his body
below the heart lengthen

and distance itself across the room
where the masked surgeon worked
with knives and clips in green mist
of a rising tide. He never slept

but dreamed of good work, loading
and splitting, hauling, cradling,
lifting, pushing, sweating. Work
and love mixed together—fuel

and glue of our days. Then the walls
of muscles tearing, insides pushing out,
a little at first, then embarrassingly,
then frighteningly. Drifting above

the body, away from the body
being repaired, walls of the temple
being restored, except for one small
tributary cut and dammed for good,

thought of all the live sperm spilled
or trapped or given into another,
love and work mixed together.
Out there in the morphine

he felt sad and then nothing—
never slept, but when it wore off
and pain came to visit the incisions
he wakened to it, almost grateful.

Rita Dove

SINGSONG

When I was young, the moon spoke in riddles
and the stars rhymed. I was a new toy
waiting for my owner to pick me up.

When I was young, I ran the day to its knees.
There were trees to swing on, crickets for capture.

I was narrowly sweet, infinitely cruel,
tongued in honey and coddled in milk,
sunburned and silvery and scabbed like a colt.

And the world was already old.
And I was older than I am today.

Frank Gaspar

SYMPOSIUM

And now what is this nonsense with my left eye?
This land-mass that drifts over whole continents of
grammar and elaboration can not be a good sign: where
is that old vigor, that hard muscle? Where are the little
stories that render me untouchable by all the conventions
of the world of things? I'm reading about Eros when
the fog comes in. I can't tell if the wet heavy air out
under the sycamores is any more a hazard to clarity
than these renegade proteins gorging on my proper sight.
The suspense is killing me: How long will Socrates take
instruction from this Diotima, this woman, on the nature of
love? Won't he turn and devour her with his characteristic
sigh when the moment is right? But now she is telling him
how Eros demands that we beget in the beautiful, how Eros
of its own nature seeks what is immortal, in flesh and soul.
Why have I waited for September for all this? Why have
I left the summer behind with the same old scattered scraps
of paper, names, numbers, instructions to myself in every
humor and discipline, injunctions to be satisfied with nothing
less than First Principles? So that a cloud may drift over my
eye? Like a wing passing over a room's lamp? Here, by my
right hand, a glass of wine and a stack of bills. Here by my
same right hand another page of penciled notes, a stale cup.
In the late hush of the hours I can hear the frogs and crickets
in the flood canals, in the city's fruitful gardens. Do I dare turn
another page? Isn't it obvious that Law is not the measure of
good and evil? I am brought this way to my own hungers nightly.
I believe they are the same as yours, more or less, for who
will love us and save us, really? How will I lift myself from
one place to another by loving what I lack? How will you?
This is the way it goes in September, one page at a time, my

just portion of earthly matter floating like a dark island in the
middle distance of my vision, the distance diminishing or growing—
impossible to tell at this hour when the world of the hedge
and the lawn and the ivy is singing, when the streets are
muffled and softened, when the lights in the sky are amazed.

Donald Hall

WITNESS

From the scratchy sleep of old age,
a ghost-gray whippoorwill wakes me
with her three-step song.
When I woke in this room as a boy,
my grandmother Kate brought me coffee
at dawn, her long gray hair
already braided over her soft face
while my grandfather Wesley milked
the sisterhood in the barn.
                              One by one
they atrophy, knees and hipjoints,
ears and eyes, leg muscles and fingers.
Hair departs from the head
and dark tight hairs from the body,
leaving a whiteness of old thighs
and calves, smooth as a girl's
but with blue veins, the wreckage
and comfort of a body contracted
to frailty.
                    We wheelbarrowed milkcans
to Route 4, where they perched
for the dairy truck as the new day rose
past Ragged Mountain, over Kearsarge.
We hayed with Riley the horse under a sun
that never moved from its noon.
                              On Sunday
the cousins visited with vivacious
red wrinkled faces, neck-wattles,
and liver spots, who waved thin hands
to conduct the familiar stories, and stood
slowly, in sections, to stretch and yawn

before walking.
                    At bedtime Wesley
gummed bread and milk
while Kate drank Moxie and we listened
to Edward R. Murrow on the Emerson
radio, shaped like a cathedral,
who told us that London was burning.
At ninety my grandmother gave up
her sheep and her chickens, to live
seven years in a diminishing house.
When she died, I entered
her oil-cloth'd kitchen to grow old
as Kate grew old, to look out
the same window at the same acres,
where in mid-afternoon the western sun
paints the unpainted wood of the barn,
ruin of gray and gold that exalts
new darkness and vanishing day.
A lamp stays lit all night
in the witness's house.
                    Each September
day is the last day, as oak branches
brush against each other, and sun
glistens on grass plated with frost
and an ankle flexes to climb the exacting hill
where Wesley trekked, late afternoon,
to fetch his cattle down.
                    Sunrise
is lavender, orange, and pink, latticing
a sky as gray and hard as ice
in the new cold. I scrape the windshield,
feeling a bite in my elbow,
to drive for the *Globe*. In the rear view
mirror the sky over Kearsarge is pink,
lavender, and orange as I drive
home, happy, to black coffee and news
of cities and fire under the standing lamp.

Marge Piercy

UP BUT NOT OVER

What does it mean to be sixty
and still wake up squirming—
something stupid I said in eighth grade.
A miscue in a party in college.

Years past when I could not sleep
I would count lovers instead
of sheep and always a decade
in the past, consciousness would fade.

Now I count unpaid bills. This
is not an improvement. Troubles
thicken like overcooked pudding.
A spoon stands up in my brain.

When I leave home, my diary
at thirteen announced, I will do
whatever I want. When I am
published, I said at twenty-five

my road will be smooth
as a satin sheet ready for sex.
Always I expected life
would get easier. It didn't.

It's uphill all the way until
the last cliff, like Half Dome
at Yosemite. Always past these
mountains are higher peaks

and rougher terrain as the light
begins to dim and the load gets
heavier. Shuffle and sigh.
The only way to go is on.

Colette Inez

THE ROLL ON THE GREAT LAWN

I saw sprouted grass flatten
as the children
rolled down the slope &
wanting that childhood
which I had rolled away
like a messy bed,
I picked a moment with no
lookers-on, the children
had spun back to town
& I lay down at the crest
of the green and sent my body
turning, turning,
until supine it collapsed
& I laughed,
dandelion floss,
bits of bark, twigs,
moss on my sagging clothes,
to see the likes
of a woman in high-middle years
neither rash nor wise,
carrying on
so strangely joyful
at the bottom of the rise.

Linda Pastan

50 Years

Though we know
how it will end:
in grief and silence,
we go about our ordinary days
as if the acts of boiling an egg
or smoothing down a bed
were so small
they must be overlooked
by death. And perhaps

the few years left, sun drenched
but without grand purpose,
will somehow endure,
the way a portrait of lovers endures
radiant and true on the wall
of some obscure Dutch museum,
long after the names
of the artist and models
have disappeared.

Carol Frost

A Woman Like Yourself

You walk toward a woman like yourself,
but older,
only she isn't. You know how that is?
It could be anywhere
(Rue de Charpentier, maybe),
and as strong a desire not to die
as anything you've felt before
darkens in your nerves. You'd need stars
in the brain
to feel your own self.
You think, her friends, the bric-a-brac
in her dressing room, blouses, even a gesture
as her daughter turns her head
will outlast her presence here,
now, by an épicerie
with its signs and elaborate fruit boxes,
Jus de pommes pour votre santé,
another language, piece-bright,
to rinse and wring the ear.
Already around the next curve
of her way, the woman goes,
and the moment means nothing
that the mind doesn't magnify.
Aren't we too real
to be otherwise? You adjust
a strand of hair behind your ear,
perhaps a sigh, a rueful glance
at your reflection in the little spot of glass
free from advertisements.
Then in your ardor,
only yours, you resume

the day, lured by something,
but as if nothing at all
happened.

David Kirby

A Man Like You But Older

Here's how you find a really good restaurant:
you go to the part of town where you want to eat,
    then you stand around till you see someone
who looks like you, or a slightly better-fed version of yourself,
        maybe, someone just a little paunchier
than you are and a year or two older and certainly
    someone more affluent than you but not much,
because after all you're thinking ahead here,

    you're looking for the person you'll be in a couple
of years, the one who *really* knows where to go
    and what to get, not the person you are now, for as much
as you love yourself, it goes without saying
        that in the future you expect to be someone
you love even more, someone you absolutely worship,
    a person you'd spend every waking moment
with if you weren't that person already.

    You certainly don't want to accost the person
you'll be in 20 years! This one is liable
    to be stove up from excesses or, by the same token,
puritanical and disapproving, a regular Savonarola,
        or maybe just someone with whom you
no longer share—I mean, don't yet share—
    enough common cultural references and therefore
with whom you can no more converse

    than I might with the self I was 27 years ago
behind the shuttered windows of the *casa di cura*
    on the Via Pietro Thouar where I stood just this afternoon,
brushing back my graying hair and squinting to see

          inside the delivery room where my younger self
wheels and holds his head in his hands and tries
       not to weep with rage and frustration: my son Will
has just been born and he isn't breathing,

       and the Italian doctor and the nurses have taken him
into another room, and I'm afraid they're going to
       bring him back dead, and my then-wife is sleeping
like a baby herself, though her blood is everywhere,
          and there's no one for me to talk to, and I am afraid
they're going to come in and hand me this dead child
       and say *Mi dispiace tanto*, and I'll say I'm sorry, too,
and then what will I say, and to whom?

       The man I finally ask about the restaurant
is a dreamy sort who is licking an ice-cream cone
       with an air of more than just a little self-satisfaction
and who answers my query with a restrained enthusiasm
          that I find charming now that I'm sitting with Barbara
in the place he recommended and waiting
       for what promises to be some excellent roast fish,
grilled vegetables, and cold wine to arrive

       and remembering how unhappy my younger self was,
the self with darker hair and perfect eyesight
       but no real worldly experience of any kind,
yet I thought I was the oldest man in the world,
          though I was just 27 myself.
And just then a nurse comes back with Will in her arms,
       and he looks like any other baby, like
a bewildered mushroom, and she hands him to me,

       and I feel his breath on my cheek, and for a moment
I am frozen, still petrified by the horror of everything
       that had almost happened, and then suddenly
something goes off inside my chest like a nova exploding
          and I feel all this *love* for the infant Will Kirby,

this bawling bunch of wrinkled protoplasm,
        but that was 27 years ago, and now Will is himself
a doctor, an American one: he started breathing

        there in Florence and kept at it and came home
in a little sling and not a coffin and drank his milk
        and ate his mashed bananas and went to school
and to med school and is himself now bringing babies back to life,
        their fathers as crazy with fear as I that day—
how I wish I had walked over and thrown back
        the shutters and looked out the window and seen
my older self there on the sidewalk, smiling and waving.

Stephen Dunn

SIXTY

Because in my family the heart goes first
and hardly anybody makes it out of his fifties,
I think I'll stay up late with a few bandits
of my choice and resist good advice.
I'll invent a secret scroll lost by Egyptians
and reveal its contents: the directions
to your house, recipes for forgiveness.
History says my ventricles are stone alleys,
my heart itself a city with a terrorist
holed up in the mayor's office.
I'm in the mood to punctuate
only with that maker of promises, the colon:
next, next, next, it says, God bless it.
As García Lorca may have written: some people
forget to live as if a great arsenic lobster
could fall on their heads at any moment.
My sixtieth birthday is tomorrow.
Come, play poker with me,
I want to be taken to the cleaners.
I've had it with all stingy-hearted sons of bitches.
A heart is to be spent. As for me, I'll share
my mulcher with anyone who needs to mulch.
It's time to give up the search for the invisible.
On the best of days there's little more
than the faintest intimations. The millennium,
my dear, is sure to disappoint us.
I think I'll keep on describing things
to ensure that they really happened.

Alicia S. Ostriker

FIFTY

This is what a fifty-
Year-old woman looks like,
Said the glamorous feminist
Journalist when they asked her
How it felt to look so young.
A good answer.
But she didn't say, and they didn't
Ask her:
Did you expect the thread
Of your rough childhood
To unwind so far
From its beginnings?
Do you perhaps wonder,
When you try to look backward
And the thread seems invisible, as if
It has been snipped, who
In the world you are,
Stranger?
Do you think: *Let's keep this thing*
Rolling, keep on fighting, keep
Up the good work,
And glare down the steel tracks of the mirror
At the approach of the enemy
Who is still miles away
But coming like a commuter train, do you
Hit your typewriter
Every day, harder
And harder, like a recalcitrant
Spoiled child, have you surrendered
The hope of the perfect
Romance, or do you grip that

Fantasy stubbornly, like a kid holding
On to a dead pet
That she knows is dead

And do you make a joke of all of this
And when the clock says *Almost*
Quitting time, do you still answer *Never?*

William Heyen

FANA AL-FANA

Islamic mystics' *fana al-fana*,
the passing away of the passing away,

as when, last night, my wife of forty years
held me & told me she loved me:

at first, I was afraid, our decades only
rootless light from dead stars,

but then my soul received her words,
& the passing away passed away.

Part 3:
Coming to the Secret Names of Stars

I begin to hear night
breathing through me promising
that death does not last forever
and teaching me
the secret names of stars

—Richard Shelton

Tricia Cherin

LAST FUCKS

The early ones are momentous
lovely in their way of course
but fraught with what the cliché
calls performance anxiety

what is really just coming to terms
with the crux of human experience
nuance, allusion, reference
here they are plain as day

what it means to be transcendent and
feral, god and animal all at once
to know finally
what the fuss is all about

I'm starting to rehearse now
the last time
the doing it after which
it will all be finally done

the last great fuck
is perhaps more poignant
than the first dear ones
the dark lust so clear now

no longer touch resents
its burden, always
carrying more than itself
many histories in every caress

even yearning is more so
because of accumulations and contexts
if ever there will be a knowing
it must be now

after all the tryouts
the dearest coupling happens
tenderness and passion finally poised
joy wisely accommodating

touch will never be more sure
or bodies more durable
they are learned now
and weighted with living and doing

in the final familiar mysteries
there is somber abandon
such good practice
for the near oblivion

Diane Wakoski

PHALAENOPSIS

*(common house plants, called Moth Orchids, because they look
like the wings of a moth or butterfly)*

It's always the myth of place.
Creeley in Majorca,
Bukowski at Santa Anita,

and this white moth orchid
        with its final set of angel wings
                fluttering against Michigan's January snow,
give me both context and contrast.

I won't be young again,
though neither will I beat against the porch light,
nor will you find me dry
and brown,
fallen on a window sill.

Winged fantasy: the orchid itself is
a California patio plant,
while I uprooted long ago.
        And now its face turning,
in window light,
hides the secret of blooming
in the wrong season,

hides orchid sex,

hides the myth of phalaenopsis,
        of moonflower and
                Sapphic light.

The truth is, the flower on the stem,
flying there since August,
        belies the brevity of bloom.
                Six months of flowering,
contrasts
with my knowledge
of appropriate
duration. Contextualizes autonomy.
That when a woman sleeps,
she never sleeps alone.
She always expands into the moth wings
of some lover, whether it's
her mortal husband

or finally Death's orchidious angel wing,
a phalaenopsis
on her window sill
in Michigan.

Colette Inez

SEVEN STAGES OF SKELETAL DECAY

0-5   Centers of ossification appear as I squall
      "wyde in this world wonderes to hear."
      The light my second amnion.
      Mother like a frog, white exhausted thighs
      precede my deciduous teeth, the better to bite
      the asylum where I didn't earn my keep.
      Ward of the state and stable criteria.

5-12 Acetabular elements join.
      Ilium, ischium, pubis,
      a little hen's breast against my hands.
      In the corpulent dark hearing children grow
      a song of bones as the moon climbed
      and ovary bells, my eggs and the moon
      tolling each month.

12-15 Epiphysial union of long bones.
      Long bones in my stride,
      glib nights, counterfeit smiles,
      trumped-up charges against what I loved.
      Years blindly eating childhood's fat.
      Knowledge like a shield
      wounds when pressed too near.

25-36 Active vault suture closing.
      Active designs in the skull.
      Delicate zippers sealing in
      the stars, interstellar dust,
      brackets of marriage, and one short birth
      shaped like a comma between two worlds.

36-50	Lipping of scapular glenoid fossa. Fossa, a ditch. I have not come to it. Fossa, an abyss. I wait for the master archeologist to dig and pick, tweezers plucking artifacts, my trail of refuse and souvenirs.
50 plus	Quasi pathological erosions of bone. The pendulum's pit. My old electrons blow their fuse. Dark pond. My mother like a frog, white exhausted thighs collapsed.
plus	What did it mean to play a xylophone of bones? An octave of stone. Delight. Decrease, bleached lips dim against my fingers closing in a stiffening fist, dumb warrior pitted against eloquent death, illiterate mulch for those whose squalls will go "wyde in this world wonderes to hear," the light their second amnion.

Jim Simmerman

WHATEVER IT IS

Near the end we'll travel as two old men
Leaning lightly on one another for support—
One of us gone a little milky-eyed,
The other a little deaf.

We'll pack what we need in a cheap valise,
Taking turns so it's not too heavy.
When one of us tires, we'll stop awhile
And build a fire to warm our hands.

You'll have then to describe to me
The woods' deep green, the cobalt sky.
I'll point you where the nighthawk calls
So that you see what I hear, so we know…

Whatever it is we come to,
We'll travel toward together.
So when we're knocked apart at last
Something of each will go with the other.

Two old men hunched to the curve of the earth
And biding a little time between them—
Here is my shoulder steady for you,
Even this long since we started the journey.

Philip Dacey

NYC

is where my mother
came into the world
and where I'll move
when I'm old in order to leave
by the same door in the universe

through which she entered.
I'll find it somehow.
People will think I'm gawking
at the tall buildings or studying
the absence of towers.

Maybe I'll nose it,
as Hamlet did the body
under the stairs. There'll be a trace
of her in the air at that spot,
something ectoplasmic,

the burn mark where she passed,
went from absolute dark
to the lighter dark
of her mother's womb.
But maybe I won't have to look at all,

and the space, like a guardian angel,
a benign void with wings, will find me,
even though before then
Broadway bakeries at dawn
will have misled me.

Angela Ball

LESS-THAN-STYLISH ENNUI

A wistful evening without much breeze, general mildness.
I can't help but watch for my bicycle, which disappeared
Some months ago. Clowns are being fired from the TV station,
And I hope they come over here.
Some people want the same old bread
As always.
I don't understand how so many of us function
With eyes of different strengths, partial dimensions.
There are no visible cats, which could mean
They are hiding. I would like
To hide, too, if it weren't so troublesome.
A bridge cut itself in half recently, as if in protest.
Ponds are fully staffed with bream, often responsive to dangling
    crickets.
I've been out of the frying pan a long time, but I can't find the fire.
I'd feel devil-may-care, but I'm pretty sure
He doesn't. I think I'll go to the lowest point in the state
And lie down.

N. Scott Momaday

To an Aged Bear

Hold hard this infirmity.
It defines you. You are old.

Now fix yourself in summer,
In thickets of ripe berries,

And venture toward the ridge
Where you were born. Await there

The setting sun. Be alive
To that old conflagration

One more time. Mortality
Is your shadow and your shade.

Translate yourself to spirit;
Be present on your journey.

Keep to the trees and waters.
Be the singing of the soil.

Stephen Dunn

A POSTMORTEM GUIDE

—For my eulogist, in advance

Do not praise me for my exceptional serenity.
Can't you see I've turned away
from the large excitements,
and have accepted all the troubles?

Go down to the old cemetery; you'll see
there's nothing definitive to be said.
The dead once were all kinds—
boundary breakers and scalawags,
martyrs of the flesh, and so many
dumb bunnies of duty, unbearably nice.

I've been a little of each.

And, please, resist the temptation
of speaking about virtue.
The seldom-tempted are too fond
of that word, the small-
spirited, the unburdened.
Know that I've admired in others
only the fraught straining
to be good.

Adam's my man and Eve's not to blame.
He bit in; it made no sense to stop.

Still, for accuracy's sake you might say
I often stopped,
that I rarely went as far as I dreamed.

And since you know my hardships,
understand they're mere bump and setback
against history's horror.
Remind those seated, perhaps weeping,
how obscene it is
for some of us to complain.

Tell them I had second chances.
I knew joy.
I was burned by books early
and kept sidling up to the flame.

Tell them that at the end I had no need
for God, who'd become just a story
I once loved, one of many
with concealments and late-night rescues,
high sentence and pomp. The truth is
I learned to live without hope
as well as I could, almost happily,
in the despoiled and radiant now.

You who are one of them, say that I loved
my companions most of all.
In all sincerity, say that they provided
a better way to be alone.

Mary Crow

LISTENING TO MAHLER

—for Gus

The last two movements slid by too fast
while my thoughts were buried in the clock
which predicts I have thirty more years

and will be older than I ever wanted to be,
yet my body volatile, never meant to walk on
waves of time or produce solitude's grammar.

Long life calls for another tongue, the first one
worn out, new syllables please, to be hope, to be
hip joint, to be gouty toe, to be stoop.

The music: strips of darkness billow and swerve,
sound smoothed as stone by white water,
room folding closer, exuberance spirals,

and I think of my body done with the thrashing,
done with the lilting air, perfect arc of notes, tugs
of phrasing, molten grief I pour into its structure.

Toi Derricotte

THE PROMISE

I will never again
expect too much of you. I have
found out the secret of marriage:
I must keep seeing your beauty
like a stranger's, like the face
of a young girl passing on a train
whose moment of knowing illumines
it—a golden letter in a book.
I will look at you in such
exaggerated moments, lengthening
one second and shrinking eternity
until they fit together like man and wife.
My pain is expectation:
I watch you for hours sleeping, expecting
you to roll over, a dead man,
and look me in the eye;
my days are seconds of waiting
like the seconds between the makings
of boiling earth and sweating rivers.
What am I waiting for if not
your face—like a fish floating
up to the surface, a known
but forgotten expression that
suddenly appears—or like myself,
in a strip of mirror, when, having
passed, I come back to that image
hoping to find the woman
missing. Why do you think I sleep
in the other room, planets away,
in a darkness where I could die solitary,
an old nun wrapped in clean white sheets?

Because of lies I sucked
in my mother's milk, because
of pictures in my first grade reader—
families in solid towns as if
the world were rooted and grew down
holding to the rocks, eternally;
because of rings in jewelers' windows

engraved with sentiments—*I love you
forever*—as if we could survive
any beauty for longer than just after...
So I hobble down a hall
of disappointments past where
your darkness and my darkness have
had intercourse with each other.
Why have I wasted my life
in anger, thinking I could have more
than what is glimpsed in recognitions?
I will let go, as we must
let go of an angel called
back to heaven; I will not hold
her glittering robe, but let it
drift above me until I see
the last shred of evidence.

Rosellen Brown

EVERYONE'S LIVES...

Everyone's lives have begun to look alike.
Jeanine Derbyfield, her hair still thick and red as a fox's,
who never said a willing word to me in school—
Jeanine-the-jock, all muscle, all desperate winner, who mocked
the rest of us for our books, our sagging gym suits, our old-lady
legs—sits in the waiting room with her mother

who looks like my mother in her white lace cap of hair,
dozing, smiling at her knees,
and we finally talk, quietly, Jeanine and I,
below the threshold of their blasted hearing.

I swear, the deeper into the muck and muddle of our particulars—
the insulin shots, the weddings, wills,
douches and rhododendrons, the pills and potato bugs, the
    bankruptcies
and valedictorians and drop-outs, the picnics and teapots and wakes—
the farther away we get.

                        No, the higher up. I feel like a pilot
flying over the tiny, separate plots of our lives,
I see how the shapes we've worked so hard at carving out and
    cultivating
to look like no one else's begin to resemble each other. At fifteen
    thousand feet,
they blend, their borders run together, vague, finally invisible.

From here, in fact, the plots became identical—Lord, those deep,
dark rectangles! Figures mill around for a while
like ants. Later, someone tucks them under a quilt of grass
and the hillside goes on again, uninterrupted.

Jeanine, holding her mother's boneless hand, must see it too: When
    someone
carves a name on a stone,
that's how we'll know it's ours.

David Citino

THE FATHER AND THE SON

I nick my chin while shaving;
my son bares his wrist,
searches for the rustiest blade,
sorrow pooling in his eyes.

I scold; he thrusts his hand
into ice, fire, calls himself
"Forever Second Best," climbs
the cross, singing "It is finished."

I grow comic; he invents love,
the erection, children.
He watches as I go ashen,
fall backwards into the casket.

We trade places; I bring flowers,
light memory's candles with
his last breath. We trade places.
This goes on forever and ever.

Peter Meinke

THE DEATH OF FRIENDS

There are those who don't believe in death
It's natural they say. God's way
recycling the universe: the breath
of jasmine *our* breath the jagged cries of jays
our cry This golden rain tree petal
floats slanting to our table here
because the ashes of our loved ones settle
deep into the DNA of everywhere

This seems both hopeful and scientific
which is to say American: I'm sick
of it Be logical until your brain turns blue
But she
will never come back. Nor he

Nor I nor you

Philip Levine

BURIAL RITES

Even on a rare morning of rain,
like this morning, with the low sky
hoarding its riches except for
a few mock tears, the hard ground
accepts nothing. Six years ago
I buried my mother's ashes
beside a young lilac that's now
taller than I, and stuck the stub
of a rose bush into her dirt,
where like everything else not
human it thrives. The small blossoms
never unfurl; whatever they know
they keep to themselves until
a morning rain or a night wind
pares the petals down to nothing.
Even the neighbor cat who shits
daily on the paths and then hides
deep in the jungle of the weeds,
refuses to purr. It's right to end up
beside the woman who bore me,
to shovel into the dirt whatever's left
and leave only a name for someone who wants it. Think of it,
my name, no longer a portion
of me, no longer inflated
or bruised, no longer stewing
in a rich compost of memory
or the simpler one of bone, kitty,
litter, the roots of the eucalyptus
I planted back in '73,
a tiny me taking nothing, giving
nothing, empty, and free at last.

Philip Dacey

Box

I imagine taking up boxing when I'm 80
so that my children can say,
when asked how I died,
Dad was killed by a
left hook in the fourth round.

No long lugubrious good-byes in the hospital.
Maybe a fall backwards
through the ropes to land
on my head ringside
at the feet of gamblers and their babes.

With my skinny legs poking out
of shiny shorts, I'd of course
have to coax and prod
the other, younger boxers: *Hit me,*
you son of a bitch, I'm not made of glass!

Heavenly peace? A bore. Better
the ring and roundhouse punches
for all eternity, bouncing in the corner
on my toes, sucking on rubber,
ready for whatever's coming next.

Short of that, how about
a stony-winged angel on guard
above my grave in a deep crouch,
both hands gloved, the right cocked,
the left jabbing the void away?

Gene Frumkin

OVER THE GREAT BARRIER

We never stop until the great barrier stops us.
Even then we try to climb over the wall. Some do
and are never heard from again, since the rest of us
live on here in perpetual dusk. What could voices
say there where nothing matters except
housekeeping? We, meanwhile, remember
those others and envy their long lives, ourselves

wishing we could have their time, as a bonus
perhaps, for having listened to their long
meanderings. We continually look for
children to replace us, prune our flowers that
go on living without reproach. But this is only
our wish. We don't know how the others
are faring beyond our telescopes. Do they hear us

and learn what is going on as our voices
grow gnarled and words clump together? Occasionally
we go to hear them under their stones, but hear
nothing. They have shut up at last, and we know
it will be no different for ourselves when time loses us
and we look for ourselves outside the great barrier.
We talk as much as we can. Silence will come.

Donald Finkel

BURDEN

Nouns were the first to slip away.
Was it because they were easier to forget,
or the most dispensable?

Funerals back then were milling
with nouns whose names he'd forgotten,
if he'd ever met them.

Evidently, somewhere out there
a swarm of improper nouns
had prospered and multiplied.

Odd nouns came knocking every day
looking for work, till the old bard
left off answering the door.

Verbs were beasts of another persuasion.
For a while some stayed behind,
pacing the halls or curled on the living room sofa.

But they had to be fed. Some nights
they sank their claws in his thigh
when they were hungry.

As the last syllable crept away,
he felt a peculiar lightness,
like the wisp that rises

from a smoldering wick—
as if words were the burden
he'd been bearing, all his life.

Li-Young Lee

STATION

Your attention please.
Train number 9, The Northern Zephyr,
destined for River's End, is now boarding.
All ticketed passengers
please proceed to the gate marked *Evening*.

Your attention please. Train number 7,
Leaves Blown By, bound for The Color of Thinking
and Renovated Time, is now departing.
All ticketed passengers may board
behind my eyes.

Your attention please. Train number 4, The Twentieth Century,
has joined The Wind Undisguised to become The Written Word.

Those who never heard their names
may inquire at the uneven margin of the story
or else consult the ivy
lying awake under our open window.

Your attention please. The Music,
arriving out of hidden ground
and endlessly beginning, is now the flower,
now the fruit, now our cup and cheer
under branches more ancient
than our grandmother's hair.

Passengers with memories of the sea
may board leisurely at any unmarked gate.

Fateful members of the foam may proceed to azalea.

Your attention please.
Under falling petals, never think about home.
Seeing begins in the dark.
Listening stills us.
Yesterday has gone
ahead to meet you.

All light-bearing tears may be exchanged
for the accomplished wine.

Your attention please. Train number 66,
Unbidden Song, soon to be
the full heart's quiet, takes no passengers.

Please leave your baggage with the attendant
at the window marked *Your Name Sprung from Hiding.*

An intrepid perfume is waging our rescue.

You may board at either end of Childhood.

Charles Wright

HAWKSBANE

There are things that cannot be written about, journeys
That cannot be taken they are so sacred and long.

There is no nature in eternity, no wind shift, no weeds.

Whatever our vision, whatever our implement,
We looked in the wrong places, we looked for the wrong things.

We are not what is new, we are not what we have found.

John Weston

Citrus Orchard

> *Christ,*
> *may I die at night.*
> > —*Robert Lowell*

I

The search for sense is senseless,
one might as well entreat the rat
breeding in the basement among jars
of marmalade, Come forth!
let us run in the temple and tip out
the cruddy fountain, ask a grapefruit
to ring like a bell, icy as a sun
somewhere beyond recall.

The saws screak. Someone
is chopping down the trees,
to be gone altogether in a week.
Paint will soon chip and crackle,
we will divest ourselves of clothes
dive into silence, unable to breathe
or hear the high morning sing.

II

The ripples subside. In the water glass
a girl gazes at her thoughts of life to come,
combing her hair the color of lemons
on the blue tiles at her feet, her breasts bare
and thin as a nymph's, but finds nothing
much to cling to, it all seems slippery

as okra which she hates or the matinee
of boys whom she might hate, too,
uncertainly, hiding in the citrus orchard
like those men in the Bible who spied on
whoever it was bathing outdoors in a tub.
She wonders if her hair will lighten
in the shouts of summer.

III

At four, two old ladies sit for tea
on their porch. Dora drinks from a cup
as fragile as the veins in her temples,
from time to time turns the gold ring
on her finger, sucks a lemon slice.
Belle, excited as a sparrow on waking,
chatters about her dream at nap time,
something to do with fog
at the bottom of their street, bricks,
a girl gone bad in the neighborhood.
The other bobs her red feathered hat,
declares there is no telling in this world,
one must be careful what one dreams.

Neither hears the frail scream
as the cat, slipping up the stairs,
lays at their satin feet a rabbit
tiny, brown and sleek. Papa
planted the orchard, Dora says,
a hundred years ago now look,
there'll be no lemon for our tea.
Yes, she ran off with a salesman
wearing a spotted tie, I saw it plain
as day, the bricks were slick with fog.

IV

Each dawn a pair of gray franklins
begins its sonata from the high branch
answered by another a half-mile away
at the sea, bell chimes and chuckle,
a falling away at last when they sail down
the heated air to feed among lost oranges,
scratch up the secret lives of dirt.

There is no silence complete,
always the hum of tires on the overpass,
an owl seeking dusk, unspeakable
twitter of caskets on the shadowed hill,
the sipping of rats hollowing
tangerines into ornamental shells.

Maxine Kumin

SUMMER MEDITATION

It isn't gunfire
that wakes me
but the rat-a-tat-tat
of hickory nuts raining
on the tin roof
of the trailer barn.
Then the barred owl
in the blackness, calling
for company, who
who cooks for you-u-u?
and suddenly
it's morning.

In the bathroom
the tiny phallic
night light
still flickers.
Black spots
of gnats, moths
folded in slumber
with one swipe
of the washcloth
reduce to powder.
An earwig to flush.
Two mosquitoes
lurking in the shower.
Killing before
breakfast

and killing after:
Japanese beetles

all green and coppery
fornicating on
the leafy tops
of the raspberries
piggybacked
triplets and foursomes
easy to flick
into soap suds.
Their glistening
drowning selves
a carpet of beads unstrung
spit Bad Buddhist!

At the pond
naked, pale
I slip between
two shores
of greenery
solitary
back in the murk
of womb while
there goes mr. big
the brookie
trailed by mrs. big
wispy silhouettes
darting in synchrony
past the deep pool
by the great rock

the great rock
that is always dark
on its underside
the one I used to dive
from, aiming to come up
in the heart
of a cold spring
rising exultant

time after time
into the fizz
of lime-green light…

At sundown the horses'
winter hay arrives.
The dogs raise
an appropriate racket.
Always the annual
hay supply comes
at suppertime
on the hottest day
of August.

Eddie and Tim, oily
with sweat, grunt
bucking hay
heaving
40-lb. bales up
crisscrossed like
Pik-up Stix
so air can circulate.
They stand around after
holding their elbows
that noncommittal
Yankee gesture
that says friendship
same as last year.
We chat, exchange
town gossip
the usual, except
Eddie's son
is in Iraq.

Afterward
the sweep-up.
Hay clings to everything

like rumor.
The full barn
cries summer, a scent
I suck into myself.
Big red sundown
induces melancholy.

I want to sing
of death unbruised.
Its smoothening.
I want to prepare
for death's arrival
in my life.
I want to be
an advanced thinker—
the will, the organ donation,
the power of attorney—
but when my old
dead horses come
running toward me
in a dream
healthy and halterless
—Gennie, Taboo, and Jack—
I take it back.

If only death could be
like going to the movies.
You get up afterward
and go out
saying, how was it?
Tell me, tell me how was it.

Harvey Shapiro

DESK

After my death, my desk,
which is now so cluttered,
will be bare wood, simple and shining,
as I wanted it to be in my life,
as I wanted my life to be.

Jean Valentine

THE WORN HAND

The worn hand

the old fin

early   late

behind the moon

the translucent people

lay like stars   luminous

on the table of space

                    first
last

they swam away

Jane Hirshfield

It Was Like This: You Were Happy

It was like this:
you were happy, then you were sad,
then happy again, then not.

It went on.
You were innocent or you were guilty.
Actions were taken, or not.

At times you spoke, at other times you were silent.
Mostly, it seems you were silent—what could you say?

Now it is almost over.

Like a lover, your life bends down and kisses your life.

It does this not in forgiveness—
between you, there is nothing to forgive—
but with the simple nod of a baker at the moment
he sees the bread is finished with transformation.

Eating, too, is a thing now only for others.

It doesn't matter what they will make of you
or your days: they will be wrong,
they will miss the wrong woman, miss the wrong man,
all the stories they tell will be tales of their own invention.

Your story was this: you were happy, then you were sad,
you slept, you awakened.
Sometimes you ate roasted chestnuts, sometimes persimmons.

Richard Shelton

OUT HERE

when the moon rises
and Sonora is covered
with silence brilliant as snow
I walk into a dream unafraid

down there in the valley
lights go on at night
but out here
the stars are alive and well
and each has a secret name

out here I am alone
but this is my country
well past the halfway point
between the past and future

out here nothing needs me
nothing fails me I lie down
in the bed of an arroyo
look at the stars and forget
first the promises
made to myself kept or broken
then the promises
made to others then my name
place of birth the numbers
and all the rest

when there is nothing left
I remember the precision
of the hummingbird piercing

the dark heart of the hibiscus
and doing no damage

I begin to hear night
breathing through me promising
that death does not last forever
and teaching me
the secret names of the stars

Acknowledgments

The editor and the Pima Press Board wish to thank Bree De Volder for her enthusiastic, thoughtful, dedicated assistance.

Permission to reprint poems is gratefully acknowledged to the following:

Addonizio, Kim. "Getting Older" from *Tell Me*. Used by permission of BOA Editions, Ltd.

Addonizio, Kim. "31-Year-Old Lover" from *What Is This Thing Called Love: Poems* (2004). Used by permission of W.W. Norton & Company, Inc.

Addonizio, Kim. "The Work" from *What Is This Thing Called Love: Poems* (2004). Used by permission of W.W. Norton & Company, Inc.

Amsden, Tim. "When I Am Old." Reprinted by permission of the author.

Ball, Angela. "Less-Than-Stylish Ennui." Reprinted by permission of the author.

Barks, Coleman. "No Finale" from *Club: Granddaughter Poems*. Maypop, Athens, Georgia, 2001. Reprinted by permission of the author.

Bly, Robert. "Looking at Aging Faces" from *Morning Poems*, HarperCollins, New York, 1997. Reprinted by permission of the author.

Brown, Rosellen. "The two of them approach..." from *Cora Fry's Pillow Book*, Farrar Straus Giroux, New York, 1994. Reprinted by permission of the author.

Brown, Rosellen. "Me buttoned..." from *Cora Fry's Pillow Book*, Farrar Straus Giroux, New York, 1994. Reprinted by permission of the author.

Brown, Rosellen. "Everyone's lives..." from *Cora Fry's Pillow Book*, Farrar Straus Giroux, New York, 1994. Reprinted by permission of the author.

Budy, Andrea Hollander. "Living Room" from *RUNES: An Anthology of Poetry*, 2004. Reprinted by permission of the author.

Budy, Andrea Hollander. "In the Sixth Year of My Father's Illness" from *RUNES: An Anthology of Poetry*, 2003. Reprinted by permission of the author.

Carter, Jefferson. "Foul Mouth" from *Litter Box*, Spork Press. Reprinted by permission of the author.

Cherin, Tricia. "Role Models." Reprinted by permission of the author.

Cherin, Tricia. "Last Fucks" from *Ambit 175*, Spring 2004. Reprinted by permission of the author.

Citino, David. "A Brief History of Fathers": *The News and Other Poems*. South Bend, Indiana. University of Notre Dame Press, 2002. Reprinted by permission of the author.

Citino, David. "The Father and the Son": *The House of Memory*. Columbus, Ohio State University Press, 1990. Reprinted by permission of the author.

Collier, Michael. "The Singer." Reprinted by permission of the author.

Collins, Billy. "Forgetness" from *Questions About Angels*, Billy Collins © 1991. Reprinted by permission of the University of Pittsburgh Press.

Cooley, Peter. "May 7, 2001." Reprinted by permission of the author.

Crow, Mary. "Listening to Mahler" from *Freshwater Review*. Reprinted by permission of the author.

Dacey, Philip. "Box." Reprinted by permission of the author.

Dacey, Philip. "NYC." Reprinted by permission of the author.

Deming, Alison H. "The Old Man." Reprinted by permission of the author.

Derricotte, Toi. "The Promise." Reprinted by permission of the author.

Dove, Rita. "Götterdämmerung" from *On The Bus With Rosa Parks*, W. W. Norton & Co., Inc., © 1999 by Rita Dove. Used by permission of W.W. Norton & Company, Inc.

Dove, Rita. "Singsong" from *On The Bus With Rosa Parks*, W. W. Norton & Co., Inc., © 1999 by Rita Dove. Reprinted by permission of the author.

Dubie, Norman. "The Mandala Keeper" from *The American Poetry Review*. Reprinted by permission of the author.

Dunn, Stephen. "Aging" from *Loosestrife*. W.W. Norton & Company, Inc. © 1996 by Stephen Dunn. Used by permission of W.W. Norton & Company, Inc.

Dunn, Stephen. "Sixty" from *Different Hours*. W.W. Norton & Company, Inc. © 2000 by Stephen Dunn. Used by permission of W.W. Norton & Company, Inc.

Edson, Russell. "The Knitting." Reprinted by permission of the author.

Evans, Mari. "The Elders." Reprinted by permission of the author.

Field, Edward. "Dead Man Walking." Reprinted by permission of the author.

Finkel, Donald. "Leavings" from *The Detachable Man* © 1984, Atheneum. Reprinted by permission of the author.

Finkel, Donald. "Burden" from *Not So The Chairs: Selected and New Poems* © 2003. Reprinted by permission of the author.

Franco, Gina. "The Keepsake Storm" from *The Keepsake Storm.* © 2004 The Arizona Board of Regents. Reprinted by permission of the University of Arizona Press.

Franco, Gina. "Paraffin Days" from *The Keepsake Storm.* © 2004 The Arizona Board of Regents. Reprinted by permission of the University of Arizona Press.

Freeman, Helen Ruth. "That Time of Year." Reprinted by permission of the author.

Frost, Carol. "A Woman Like Yourself." Reprinted by permission of the author.

Frumkin, Gene. "Being Old, Still Playing." Reprinted by permission of the author.

Frumkin, Gene. "Over the Great Barrier." Reprinted by permission of the author.

Gallagher, Tess. "She Wipes Out Time." Reprinted by permission of the author.

Gaspar, Frank. "Symposium." Reprinted by permission of the author.

Gilbert, Sandra M. "A Sundowner." Reprinted by permission of the author.

Gioia, Dana. "The Lost Garden." Reprinted by permission of the author.

Greenberg, Alvin. "car talk: the 16-valve engine, spluttering." Reprinted by permission of the author.

Hall, Donald. "Witness." Reprinted by permission of the author.

Hamill, Sam. "To Hayden Carruth on His Eightieth Birthday." Reprinted by permission of the author.

Hamill, Sam. "After Han Yu." Reprinted by permission of the author.

Hamill, Sam. "The Orchid Flower." Reprinted by permission of the author.

Harper, Michael S. "HEADSET (in memory of my mother)." Reprinted by permission of the author.

Hecht, Anthony. "Sarabande on Attaining the Age of Seventy-seven" from *Collected Later Poems*, © by Anthony Hecht. Used by permission of Alfred A. Knopf, a division of Random House, Inc.

Heyen, William. "American Time" from *The Host: Selected Poems 1965-1990*, © 1994 by Time Being Books. Used by permission of Time Being Books.

Heyen, William. "Fana Al-Fana." Reprinted by permission of the author.

Hirsch, Edward. "Cold Calls." Reprinted by permission of the author.

Hirsch, Edward. "The Chardin Exhibition." Reprinted by permission of the author.

Hirshfield, Jane. "It Was Like This: We Were Happy" first published in *The New Yorker*. Reprinted by permission of the author.

Hirshfield, Jane. "The Gallop" from *Given Sugar, Given Salt*, HarperCollins. © 2001 by Jane Hirshfield. Reprinted by permission of HarperCollins Publishers.

Hirshfield, Jane. "This Was Once A Love Poem" from *Given Sugar, Given Salt*, HarperCollins. © 2001 by Jane Hirshfield. Reprinted by permission of HarperCollins Publishers.

Hoagland, Tony. "Behind Time." Reprinted by permission of the author.

Hollander, John. "…And S.B. Whitebait, Who Was Well Over Sixty." Reprinted by permission of the author.

Hongo, Garrett. "Elegy, Kahuku." Reprinted by permission of the author.

Inez, Colette. "The Roll on the Great Lawn." Reprinted by permission of the author.

Inez, Colette. "Seven Stages of Skeletal Decay." Reprinted by permission of the author.

Jarman, Mark. "Song of Roland" from *To the Green Man*, Sarabande Books, 2004. Reprinted by permission of the author.

Kennedy, X. J. "Leave of Absence," revised version of a poem in *Nude Descending a Staircase*. Carnegie Mellon University Press. © 1994, 2005 by X. J. Kennedy. Reprinted by permission of the author.

Kennedy, X. J. "Old Men Pitching Horseshoes" from *Cross Ties: Selected Poems*. University of Georgia Press. © by X. J. Kennedy. Reprinted by permission of the author.

Kirby, David. "A Man Like You But Older." Reprinted by permission of the author.

Koertge, Ron. "Old People." Reprinted by permission of the author.

Koertge, Ron. "55" from *Geography of the Forehead*. University of Arkansas Press. Reprinted by permission of the author.

Kowit, Steve. "Cosmetics Do Not Good." Reprinted by permission of the author.

Krysl, Marilyn. "Last Wish." Reprinted by permission of the author.

Kumin, Maxine. "The Final Poem." Reprinted by permission of the author.

Kumin, Maxine. "Summer Meditation" from *Jack and Other New Poems*. W.W. Norton & Company, Inc. © 2005 by Maxine Kumin. Used by permission of W.W. Norton & Company, Inc.

Ladinsky, Daniel. "From Hafiz on Aging…" © Daniel Ladinsky 2005. Reprinted by permission of the author.

Laux, Dorianne. "Singing Back the World." Used by permission of BOA Editions, Ltd.

Laux, Dorianne. "Ghosts." Used by permission of BOA Editions, Ltd.

Laux, Dorianne. "After Twelve Days of Rain." Used by permission of BOA Editions, Ltd.

Lee, Li-Young. "Station." Reprinted by permission of the author.

Levine, Philip. "Burial Rights" from *The New Yorker*, Spring 2005. Reprinted by permissionof the author.

Lieberman, Laurence. "Hoisting Jewel." Reprinted by permission of the author.

Liu, Timothy. "Between Youth and Death." Reprinted by permission of the author.

Locklin, Gerald. "Richard Diebenkorn: *Girl Smoking*." Reprinted by permission of the author.

Mairs, Nancy. "Through Time." Reprinted by permission of the author.

Mariani, Paul. "Fear" from *Death and Transfigurations: Poems*, © 2005 Paul Mariani. Used by permission of Paraclete Press.

Pape, Greg. "Morphine" from *American Flamingo Poems*, © 2005 by Greg Pape. Reproduced by permission Southern Illinois University Press.

Pastan, Linda. "Don't Think of This" from *The Gettysburg Review*. Reprinted by permission of the author.

Pastan, Linda. "50 Years" from *Witness*. Reprinted by permission of the author.

Piercy, Marge. "The lived in look." © Marge Piercy 2004. Reprinted by permission of the author.

Piercy, Marge. "Dislocation." © 2003 Marge Piercy. Reprinted by permission of the author.

Piercy, Marge. "Up but not over." © Marge Piercy 2003. Reprinted by permission of the author.

Plumly, Stanley. "Silent Heart" from *The Atlantic Monthly*. Reprinted by permission of the author.

Ray, David. "Charlotte the Centenarian" © 2005 by David Ray. Reprinted by permission of the author.

Ray, Judy. "Naming." Reprinted by permission of the author.

Ray, Judy. "Time Divided." Reprinted by permission of the author.

Rickel, Boyer. "Two Dreams of a Son in Middle Age" from *Prairie Schooner*. Reprinted by permission of the author.

Roberts, Len. "Monitoring Impulses" from *The American Poetry Review*, 2001. Reprinted by permission of the author.

Rogers, Pattiann. "Into the Wind's Castle" from *Generations*, Penguin, 2004. Reprinted by permission of the author.

Rogers, Pattiann. "In Union: Skinny Grandfather Riding a Bicycle" from *Generations*, Penguin, 2004. Reprinted by permission of the author.

Rogers, Pattiann. "Watching the Ancestral Prayers of Venerable Others" from *Song of the World Becoming, New and Collected Poems, 1981-2001*, Milkweed Editions, 2001. Reprinted by permission of the author.

Root, William Pitt. "The End of Winter in an Old Neighborhood" from *Trace Elements from a Recurring Kingdom*. Reprinted by permission of the author.

Root, William Pitt. "Passing Go" from *Trace Elements from a Recurring Kingdom*. Reprinted by permission of the author.

Shapiro, Harvey. "The Librarian" from *St. Anne's Review*. Reprinted by permission of the author.

Shapiro, Harvey. "The Old Poet Sums Up." Reprinted by permission of the author.

Shapiro, Harvey. "Desk" from *Hanging Loose*. Reprinted by permission of the author.

Shelton, Richard. "Three Poems for a Twenty-fifth Anniversary." Reprinted by permission of the author.

Shelton, Richard. "The Language of Postcards." Reprinted by permission of the author.

Shelton, Richard. "Out Here." Reprinted by permission of the author.

Simmerman, Jim. "Take What You Want but Eat What You Take" from *Moon Go Away, I Don't Love You No More*, Miami University Press, 1994. Reprinted by permission of the author.

Simmerman, Jim. "Whatever It Is" from *Once Out of Nature*, The Galileo Press, Ltd. 1989. Reprinted by permission of the author.

Simon, Maurya. "St. Paula, Before Her Death." Reprinted by permission of the author.

Simon, Maurya. "Theme and Variation" from *Days of Awe*, Copper Canyon Press, 1989. Reprinted by permission of the author.

Simpson, Louis. "Grand Forks." Reprinted by permission of the author.

Smith, Thomas R. "Daffodils for Aunt Vic" from *The Dark Indigo Current*, Holy Cow! Press, Duluth, 2000, © 2000 Thomas R. Smith. Reprinted by permission of the author.

Snodgrass, W. D. "Pacemaker" from *Poetry*. Reprinted by permission of the author.

Snodgrass, W. D. "Lasting" from *The Southern Review*, 2004. Reprinted by permission of the author.

Snodgrass, W.D. "An Envoi, Post-Turp" from *Each in His Season*. Reprinted by permission of BOA Editions, Ltd.

Soto, Gary. "Afternoon Memory" from *New and Selected Poems*, Chronicle Books, 1995. Reprinted by permission of the author.

Soto, Gary. "In time..." from *Natural Man*, Chronicle Books, 1999. Reprinted by permission of the author.

St. John, David. "Grace Harbour." Reprinted by permission of the author.

Stanton, Maura. "The Art of French Cooking." Reprinted by permission of the author.

Stanton, Maura. "Artificial Tears" from *The Formalist*, Vol. 11, Issue 2, 2000. Reprinted by permission of the author.

Stern, Gerald. "Sink" from *American Sonnets*, W.W. Norton & Co., Inc., 2002. Reprinted by permission of the author.

Williams, C.K. "Old Man." Reprinted by permission of the author.

Wilson, Keith. "The Arrival of My Mother" from *Bosque Redondo*. Reprinted by permission of the author.

Wilson, Keith. "The Old Man and His Snake" from *Lion's Gate*. Reprinted by permission of the author.

Wright, Charles. "Hawksbane." Reprinted by permission of the author.

Zolynas, Al. "My Father, at the Age of Eighty-three, Shows Up at the Family Reunion, Sporting an Amazing Beard." Reprinted by permission of the author.

Printed in the United States
39460LVS00004B/103-558